AUGUSTA TABOR

A Pioneering Woman

Augusta Tabor

AUGUSTA TABOR

A Pioneering Woman

Betty Moynihan

CORDILLERA PRESS, INC.

Publishers in the Rockies

Library of Congress Cataloging-in-Publication Data

Moynihan, Betty.
    Augusta Tabor, a pioneering woman / Betty Moynihan. — 1st ed.
       p.   cm.
    Bibliography: p.
    Includes index.
    ISBN: 0-917895-23-1 : $7.95
    1. Tabor, Augusta, d. 1895. 2. Pioneers — Colorado — Pikes
Peak Region — Biography. 3. Women pioneers — Colorado —
Pikes Peak Region — Biography. 4. Pikes Peak Region (Colo.) —
Gold discoveries. 5. Frontier and pioneer life — Colorado —
Pikes Peak Region.
    I. Title.
F782.P63M68 1988   88-14962
978.8'56 — dc19   CIP

*Cover painting: "The Rocky Mountains." Currier & Ives, 1866.
Courtesy of Denver Public Library, Western History Department.*

*Cover design by Richard M. Kohen, Shadow Canyon Graphics.
Typography and design by Shadow Canyon Graphics.*

First Edition
1 2 3 4 5 6 7 8 9
Printed in the United States of America
ISBN: 0-917895-23-1

Cordillera Press, Inc., P.O. Box 3699, Evergreen, Colorado 80439
(303) 670-3010

Contents

Acknowledgements

The research involved in this biography has been lengthy and laborious. Many have helped me. I would like to thank especially the staff of every library and museum across the continent where I worked, from Huntington Library in San Marino, California, to the Hubbard Free Library in Hallowell, Maine, as well as similar institutions in London and Paris. I am especially grateful to Catherine Engel of the Colorado Historical Society Library who helped me consistently through the years.

Likewise, thanks go to the Colorado Humanities Program, Odette Touraud, Philippe and Jeanine Laforgue, Olivier and Evelyn Laforgue, Gil Mahaffey, Harper Orahood, Duane Smith, Tom Noel, Georgina Brown, Lois Brooks, Francis and Freda Rizzari, Kay Snell, Wellena Tschamber, John Hale, Zoe Alexander, Jack Akin, Irene Bailey, Peggy DuCharme, David Parry, Stan Oliner, David Halaas, Judge Karen Metzger, Dr. Joe Zirrolli, Gary Hale, Father Michael Chamberlain, Sister Ann (Walter), Paul Hallett, Mike and Judy Dowd, Walt Borneman, and Jay Fell.

Special appreciation goes to my husband Jim, who played many roles in this involved scenario. As chauffeur, sounding board, and fellow researcher, he was always available, generously adapting his schedule to the demands of this project.

Why Augusta Tabor?

In 1978, I began writing for the *High Timber Times* (Conifer, Colorado), a weekly column that revolved around local history. I was delighted to find that among the famous people who had once lived in this area were Horace Tabor, the silver king, and his first wife Augusta. In doing research for those segments that would feature the Tabors, I discovered to my dismay that while much had been written about Horace and his second wife Baby Doe, there were few details about the life of Augusta.

This lack of information intrigued me. Augusta had come in 1859 to what is now Colorado, and as a trail blazer she deserved a special place of honor in the annals of western history. Why had she been ignored? There seemed to be two possible reasons. She may have been so scurrilous a subject that writers considered her unappetizing fare; that seemed unlikely since her pioneer status should have dwarfed any possible deficiency. Apparently, she had been purposely relegated to oblivion. Why? My terrier instincts were aroused. Once I had picked up the scent, I followed every clue trying to sniff out the truth.

When I had exhausted the files of the Western History Department of the Denver Public Library and all the resources of the Colorado Heritage Center, I was left with a mere handful of notes, most of them in conflict. How was it possible that basic facts had never been checked? Dates for birth and death are among the easiest statistics to verify. Yet not only had Augusta's death (January 30, 1895) been reported incorrectly, but also her simple tombstone in Riverside Cemetery was in error by two years.

As my search continued, the inaccuracies and half-truths multiplied. The picture of Augusta painted by the few commentators who had put their opinions in print was invariably uncomplimentary. She was supposed to have been "cold," "penurious," and "strait-laced." But I came across numerous contemporary accounts of Augusta's generosity and kindness. I documented many instances of her liberality and compassion. And references to her as a frigid New England matron were strongly at odds with Horace's accusation of adultery in the first suit he brought for divorce.

Obviously, my task was to dig in virgin territory. I realized that I would have to visit at least three other states: Maine, where Augusta was born; Kansas, where she and Horace shared their first married years; and California, where she died. The most difficult challenge would be to locate any of Augusta's direct descendants.

Fortunately, I received a grant from the Colorado Humanities Program to help with the financing. Crucial additional help was provided by two friends, Odette Touraud and Gil Mahaffey, both of whom were instrumental in my bonanza find of the Tabor heirs.

Newspaper files from the 1960s indicated that one of the great-grandchildren of Horace and Augusta had been interviewed in Denver. Philippe Laforgue, a native of France, had arrived in Colorado for a visit and had been bitterly disappointed to find so little information about Augusta. Here was my kindred spirit. Now, how to find him? The news item merely indicated that he was living in Versailles, France.

Since my first class in high school French, I had been corresponding with Odette Touraud Labrosse, a talented Parisian. In my dilemma I turned to her, confident of her interest, empathy, and efficiency. Using the telephone and local community files, Odette eventually located the correct Laforgue family. Without her help and the courteous approach she made to these strangers, my task would have been insurmountable.

Philippe Laforgue, in responding to my request, was most gracious. Yes, he had early photographs of his great-grandmother, and several other items of interest, including a diary and some scrapbooks. The next step was imperative — to meet with Philippe and copy these family treasures.

Here my friend and fellow teacher, Gil Mahaffey, played the accommodating angel. As founder and president of Voyageurs International, he made arrangements for my flight to France. In June 1983, I became a member of one of his tours to Europe.

I shall never forget an afternoon in late June in the fashionable residence of the Laforgues when Philippe handed me a photograph of the young Augusta. What joy to see at last the likeness of an attractive young woman! The pictures of Augusta available in Colorado showed her in late years after arduous living and a lifetime of labor had altered and aged her physical appearance.

In talking about the Tabors' only son, Maxcy, Philippe commented that his grandfather was "the kindest man I ever knew." Philippe manifests the same gentility. He and his family showed me the courtesy and consideration characteristic of innate refinement. I saw in them the true personality of the woman of my quest.

In his introduction to Joanne Stratton's book, *Pioneer Women*, Arthur Schlesinger, Jr. wrote, ". . . women have constituted the most spectacular casualty of traditional history. They have made up at least half of the human race; but you could never tell that by looking at the books historians write. The forgotten man is nothing to the forgotten woman." Augusta Tabor is one of the prime casualties. She bore the stamp of all enterprising adventurers who accompanied their husbands and families into the uncompromising and uncultivated hinterlands. These women came and they stayed. Their courage and determination were the foundations of a nation rich in beauty and opulent in opportunity.

Unfortunately, most people know about the Tabors only from the Baby Doe story. That is most regrettable. The shared life of Baby Doe and Horace Tabor is tarnished tinsel. It is a tawdry tale sold with Hollywood hype to an unsuspecting public. The real romance in the life of the Tabors is the saga of challenge and discovery lived by Horace and Augusta as they forged new paths into the Rocky Mountain ranges.

I
Downeast Origins

The time was 1853. The place was Augusta, capital city of the State of Maine.

Mr. William B. Pierce, building contractor, boarded a train that was heading south and west toward Massachusetts. It was an act of destiny.

What Mr. Pierce wanted were stonecutters for his quarry. What Mr. Pierce got, by the free fall of fate, was a son-in-law who would alter the future of most of his large family and give history one of its most courageous female pioneers. Whether the end result for his family was good or ill, who can say? We can say that the Pierce children by migrating from Maine to the Rocky Mountains became colonizers who left their imprint on the newly formed foundations of the great American West.

Maine lies at the northeastern tip of the United States. Once claimed by Massachusetts, it became a state in 1820. Its beauty is defined by rugged mountains that support extensive verdant forests which have given Maine the title "Pine Tree State." Its major rivers flow full and forceful toward the Atlantic Ocean, which through centuries has carved a ragged coastline. In 1853, Maine was not an easy place in which to live, but with plentiful woods, facilities for shipbuilding, fish-filled streams, and hillsides ripe with rock and gorged with granite, it did provide a good livelihood for its citizens.

Augusta was a city whose beginnings dated back to 1628. It was situated on the Kennebec River, where the winds blew plentifully and with persistence. That made the people taciturn, their voices vanquished by the bluster of such breezes. Cold, snow, fog, and driving rain tested the mettle of the inhabitants, making them resilient under duress and adaptable to adversity. People raised in this section of the country tended to be sharp of tongue and wit, determined of will, blunt of manner, clear-eyed, and clean-living.

This was the locale where the Pierce family had settled. Mr. Pierce owned more than 100 acres of land east of Church Hill Road. Here he had dug and dredged the livelihood that supported his wife and children in relative comfort. Like his father before him, William B. Pierce was a stonemason. He had left his mark on several major buildings in the capital city, but he had accomplished his primary work at the State Asylum for the Insane. When a destructive fire in 1850 demolished many of the original buildings, Mr. Pierce was appointed chief contractor and was put in charge of hiring and directing the labor force. Stone and granite Mr. Pierce had in full supply, as well as the first derrick ever used in that area. Of laborers, Mr. Pierce had not enough.

That was the reason he had boarded a train out of town — to search for stonemasons. Once on board, Mr. Pierce made the acquaintance of two brothers who were out of work and in need of employment. These brothers were John (sometimes known as Jonathan) and Horace Tabor. After some discussion, the three men reached an agreement on terms of service. Then employer and employees left the train, reversed their direction, and returned to Augusta, where the newly hired stonemasons became part of the Pierce Company.

Greeting the newcomers at the tidy Pierce residence was the wife and mother Lucy (Eaton), a pleasant helpmate who had produced offspring with tidal regularity until in 1853 the family numbered seven daughters and three sons. In those days when women were restricted to the home and were deemed of less value than men, it might have proved an embarrassment to have so many girls in the family. However,

Mr. Pierce was quite content with his recurrent blessings. His oldest daughter Rebecca had recently married Peter J. Folsom, one of his employees. That was one way of recruiting and keeping stonemasons. His second daughter was Melvina. To her Mr. Pierce entrusted the clerical and bookkeeping chores of the business. No man could have been more competent or more trustworthy.

Augusta Pierce, born March 29, 1833, was the third daughter, and she was chronically ill. Her body lacked the basic "get up and go" of a healthy child. The fact that she "went" at all was due to determination, stubbornness, and will. Mr. Pierce knew that Augusta could do anything she'd thought on and decided in favor of. Despite poor health, she had reached the age of twenty apparently through a daily struggle that had strengthened her body and spirit.

The remaining girls were Vesta, eighteen; Ruthe, seventeen; Mary, eleven; and Lilly, nine. The boys in the family consisted of Edwin, fifteen; Frank, thirteen; and the baby, seven-year-old Fred.

Mr. Pierce's closest neighbors were also liberal-minded men holding progressive views on the value and rights of women. The Reverend John Ingraham was a minister of the Universalist-Unitarian Church. The Pierces were members of his congregation. This church did not hold with fundamentalist doctrine which placed Eve and all her descendants in subservience to lord and master Adam. The Reverend Ingraham's wife was Abigail, youngest daughter of Judge Daniel Cony. So convinced was Judge Cony of the worth of women that in 1815 he started and endowed at his own expense the Cony Female Academy, a school devoted exclusively to women's education. Thanks to such tolerant, liberal neighbors and friends, Augusta grew up sure of her self-worth and confident that she was the equal of men.

The Tabor brothers had been raised in Holland, Vermont, an inconspicuous community near the Canadian border, whose first permanent settlers arrived about 1800. John and Horace had an older brother Lemuel and a younger sister Emily.

The tiny hamlet in which the Tabor family lived had few vocational opportunities for men. There was some logging, short-season farming, and a poorly paying lye industry. Sawmills operated steadily and lumber companies managed to survive. Dairy farming and maple syrup production were limited to individual families.

Horace Tabor summed up his early life: "Pa had a small farm. My people were poor. They raised wheat, potatoes, and oats, barley, and peas. Mom died of measles. The whole family, except Pa, had measles at the time. I was 16 when Mom died. My father married his second wife and [she] made it pretty hot around my ears. I left home at 19." That was in 1849. He followed his older brother John to Quincy, Massachusetts, where they both learned the stonecutters' trade. The brothers were in agreement that there was no future for them in Vermont. They were both enterprising young men, willing to work and open to opportunities. Horace was easy-going and very likable to all except those irritated by his tendency toward laziness and dreaming, characteristics that aggravated his relationship with his foster mother.

While they were living in Quincy, the brothers became acquainted with Amos Lawrence, the abolitionist. Lawrence, along with Eli Thayer, a wealthy legislator, and others of like political persuasion had started the New England Emigrant Aid Company. The primary purpose of this organization was to send people dedicated to the anti-slavery cause into Kansas Territory so that when it achieved statehood, it would enter the Union free, not slave. The company promised transportation to Kansas, lots upon which to build houses, and the availability of some type of livelihood. John and Horace Tabor believed in free state policies, and they saw this as an opportunity for advancement and adventure. But it would have to wait.

At the time they entered the employ of William Pierce, John was twenty-six years old; Horace, twenty-three. Since he was anxious to begin the western sojourn, John put in less than a year with the Pierce Company. He started out with the first group of emigrants sponsored by Eli Thayer's organization. He settled in the town that became known as Lawrence, Kansas, and urged his brother to follow him.

In the meantime, Horace became interested in Augusta Louise Pierce. She was not the prettiest of the girls. Her beauty was tenuous; she was skinny rather than slender. Her enthusiasm and drive, however, gave vitality and charm to her features. She also possessed a rich crowning glory — a head of heavy, curly brown hair. Whatever the attraction, the two young people spent hours together and seemed to

4

enjoy each other's company. Possibly, Horace saw in Augusta a complement to his own more pliant nature. She proved an incentive for him
to curb his drinking, which he claimed was an inherited weakness.
Horace approved her liberated attitude concerning female capabilities
and potential. He deemed himself a forward-looking man. A like-
minded wife should prove an asset.

While John was settling into frontier life in Kansas Territory and
taking part in the burgeoning Free Soil organization in Lawrence,
Horace was still considering the advisability of moving westward. He
received encouragement and approval from Augusta. Finally, in 1855,
Horace made the decision to join his brother. When Horace departed
from Maine, he left the Pierce household with the understanding that
if prospects out West looked agreeable, he would return to marry
Augusta.

Not long after Horace embarked for the West, the Pierce family
suffered its first loss — the close-knit group struggled to accept the
death of Vesta in her twentieth year. When Rebecca gave birth to a
daughter the following year, the child was promptly christened Vesta.
Vesta Folsom was later to appear frequently in Colorado as the pretty
and popular companion of her Aunt Augusta.

Once united in Kansas Territory, the Tabor brothers became involved
in several encounters between pro- and anti-slavery forces, even joining
John Brown, the abolitionist, in some of his forays against resident
slaveholders. Since the federal government had not endorsed Free
State policies, such activities were considered treason. For his part in
these raids, John was for a time imprisoned. Horace, born under a
luckier star than his brother, received only commendation and thanks
from his neighbors. They elected him their spokesman to the First
Kansas Free State Legislature, which convened in Topeka. This first
political office was a rehearsal for Horace's later roles in local and
state government in Colorado.

In Kansas, John had chosen to take permanent residence in Lawrence
on lots provided by the Emigrant Aid Company. Horace instead sought
farmland on which to settle. He joined a group of New Englanders
who homesteaded in Zeandale, a community about seventy miles northwest of Lawrence. The evident leader of this settlement was Josiah

Pillsbury, a man of keen intellect but frail body.

During his two years in Kansas, from 1855 to 1857, Horace Tabor appeared several times before the Topeka legislature representing the views of his neighbors and constituents in Zeandale. He also preempted a quarter section (160 acres) of farmland. The future looked promising, and Horace was confident of his ability to prosper in this new environment. Early in 1857, he returned to Maine and the Pierce household. With a loving and dedicated wife by his side, how could he fail to be successful?

On January 31, 1857, Horace (then twenty-six) and Augusta (twenty-three) were married. The Reverend John Ingraham, friend, neighbor, and minister, conducted the service, which was held in the living room where the bridal couple had first been introduced. The weather that day may have been prophetic of the difficult years to come. One of the worst snowstorms on record swirled about the capital city. The thermometer at the State Insane Asylum registered forty-two degrees below zero.

The weather did not chill the festivities. Augusta was radiant with joy; Horace basked in the admiring warmth of his in-laws' welcome. For Augusta, it was an especially fateful day, although she undoubtedly was unaware of the true implications of her choice.

As it did for every woman in those days, marriage robbed Augusta of her legal rights and individual identity. Signing the marriage contract was instant civil death for her. Laws made by men decreed that in the marriage bond two people became one. Henceforth, the wife existed only as the handmaid of her husband. He would hold all property in his name alone; moneys earned by their joint effort would be entirely his.

Totally enraptured in the bliss of the moment, Augusta penned her name to the marriage contract. Now her person, her time, her services became the sole property of Horace Austin Warner Tabor. Willingly, unselfishly, Augusta surrendered these birthrights into her husband's hands. In exchange, Horace gave her his name. At such a price, Augusta intended to keep that name forever.

After the wedding day, the couple remained with Augusta's family until the last week in February. In saying goodbye to this warm family group, Augusta first realized how pervasively her new status would affect the values and tenor of her life. Surely, there would be gain in this new vocation, but would it ever compensate for the loss of these cherished companions of her childhood?

Horace and Augusta journeyed west to Charleston, Vermont, where they witnessed the marriage of brother John to his cousin Hannah. Then the two couples and Emily Tabor entrained for Kansas Territory. In those days, dangers threatened and discomforts afflicted all travelers. But to these eager young people, drawbacks were a challenge and the future with its uncertainties appeared more enticing than the past with its known deficiencies.

II
Two Years in Kansas

With her marriage, Augusta left behind the solemn little girl who had been indulged and cosseted by her more robust sisters and brothers. With so many willing hands available, and hired help as well, Augusta had escaped many routine chores. She had never learned to cook. Now she must assume a woman's role. She intended to share equally with her husband in setting up and maintaining a new household.

Horace explained his dreams to Augusta and enlarged the horizons of her hopes. She had thought that the entire world was encompassed within the Pierce homestead and that all life was nurtured by the munificence of her native Maine. Anything beyond the city of Portland was a foreign continent.

As the newlyweds traveled away from familiar environs, Augusta began to realize the vast reaches of her country and to appreciate its incredible beauty and the extent of its riches. Niagara Falls was a colossal cascade that washed the memory of her Maine waterways into feeble trickles. Albany, Detroit, and St. Louis were cities more advanced and populous than her own native town.

The five Tabors traveled by train for about a week. Railroad travel at that time was primitive and precarious. Railroad cars were narrow wooden structures pulled by a small, cinder-belching engine that clattered and chugged along rough, unballasted tracks. The rails were light iron. The straight-of-way was interrupted by many sharp and dangerous curves. Livestock were free to wander along the tracks, provoking the engineer's patience and upsetting the advertised time schedule. Ten to twenty miles an hour was maximum speed. The coaches were sooty and foul-smelling. The seats were hard and uncomfortable. Cars were cold in winter and hot in summer. At nearly every important terminus it was necessary to transfer passengers and baggage from one railroad line to another. Frequently, these stations or depots were as much as a mile apart. Riders became walkers, impeded by their own luggage. There were no sleeping cars or dining cars, and the meals obtainable at railroad counters were distasteful both to palate and purse.

In St. Louis, the Tabors transferred to a crowded Missouri River steamboat. These boats were known to snag on underwater hazards or to end up on sandbars if the water ran low. Sometimes, passengers were forced to walk along the banks of the river while the crew tried to maneuver the boat, lightened of its load, through the shallows. When the Tabors finally arrived at Westport (now Kansas City), the party separated. John, Hannah, and Emily took the steamer *Lightfoot* to Lawrence, Kansas. Horace and Augusta stayed in Westport long enough to purchase a yoke of oxen, a wagon, some farming tools, and a quantity of seed for planting.

Their route to Zeandale, more than one hundred miles due west, was through newly settled, windblown Kansas Territory. Two friends from Maine, Samuel B. Kellogg and Nathaniel Maxcy, now appeared in the entourage. It is not clear whether they met up with the Tabors in Westport or whether they had shared most of the journey with them. Since the roads out of Westport were not entirely safe for a free-state sympathizer traveling alone with his wife, the company of these two men was warranted as well as welcome. Although the abolitionists arrived in "Bleeding Kansas" thinking themselves crusaders, they were despised as penniless busybodies by settlers whose wealth depended on the system of black indenture. While passing through pro-slavery towns, Augusta guided the oxen while the men marched alongside the wagon, their guns at the ready. Daily rains had made the road all but impassable, and bogging down in the mud was a constant time waster and temper tester. The travelers took two weeks to complete the journey.

The town of Zeandale was located along Deep Creek, where the river bottom land promised excellent farming. The name was formed from the Greek "zea" and the English "dale" describing a valley of corn. Josiah Pillsbury had chosen the site because of its natural beauty and the fordability of the stream at this particular point. He had likewise given the town its name. The New England settlers helped each other with home construction. They put up buildings with speed rather than architectural absolutes. The houses were functional and far from fashionable.

On April 19, 1857, Augusta saw her new home for the first time. It stood lonesome on a wide prairie. There was no sound of human activity, only the sad sighing of a perpetual wind. The view was unobstructed for miles. Augusta could look farther and see less than in any other place she had ever been. There was nothing but barren waste. The emptiness was not relieved but rather emphasized by a single dwelling — a twelve- by sixteen-foot cabin made of black walnut logs. There was not a single flower or colored weed to brighten the austere entrance. Just as dreary was the inside of the house. No picture, no paint gladdened the somber wooden walls. In the center of the room stood an iron cookstove, its black surface shrouded like a penitent in ashes. A wooden bed cowered in the corner, ashamed of its soiled sole adornment, a dirty tick filled with field grass. The only other item in the room was a dented, peeling trunk where Horace stored his "possibles."

Suddenly, Augusta was overwhelmed. The last two weeks had been particularly difficult. When Hannah and Emily left them in Westport, Augusta for the first time in her life was bereft of female companionship. In three short months she had gone from a pampered existence to sharing and shouldering the duties and demands of the frontier. Disappointment, disillusionment, and loneliness shattered the mask of her maturity. Childish fears surfaced. Her small frame crumpled onto the battered trunk, and she wept bitter, bitter tears.

Unsure of how to handle such abject sorrow, the men occupied themselves by emptying the wagon. Horace distracted himself by fashioning some three-legged stools, a table, and a shelf for dishes. Soon the sobbing ended, and Augusta mustered her courage. With grit she had grappled with a debilitating illness. That same grit would see her through this new affliction.

Making the house more habitable was her first priority. Under the bed she found some old copies of the *New York Tribune*. Making a paste of flour and water, she began plastering the walls, keeping the sheets upright, for she correctly guessed that these would be the only reading material she would have for months to come. Now the main task confronted her. She had to make the first real meal she had ever prepared in all her life. Mama was not there to direct her; her little sisters could not lend help and encouragement. And there were two guests to judge her efforts! She did the best she could, but she knew that if it had not been for their huge, youthful appetites, the fare would have seemed poor indeed.

What made the dinner acceptable was the touch of elegance that she added from her trousseau to this somber scene of poverty. Salt pork and beans served with sterling silver on a spotless linen cloth which camouflaged a rough plank table was an incongruity that spiced low comedy rather than high pathos. With laughter and good fellowship, the newlyweds and their Maine companions, Nathaniel and Samuel, completed their first day in the pitiful, primitive homestead.

Augusta's housewifely rituals were the symbol of everything women brought to the uncultivated West. The men who left civilization in quest of wealth and adventure accepted the land on its own terms. The women adapted to the circumstances, changing and improving what they found. Like a tablecloth thrown over roughhewn logs, they spread over the wild and wanton countryside a veneer of Eastern culture and respectability. They put the printed word where all could see it and recognize its worth. They nurtured the body and spirit of their exploring men, sustaining them as they struggled to subdue the wilderness. The women personified those values that men must transplant and honor in the course of establishing a new civilization.

The knives and forks that Augusta set upon her rude table were instruments of social grace. They would last through the turbulence of a lifetime on the frontier. They survived as all things of true value survive. When Augusta died, several pieces of this tableware remained among her effects. On these dozen pieces of solid silver the initials "ALP" of her maiden name could still be seen.

In the single room of this prairie home, there was obviously no place for Samuel Kellogg and Nathaniel Maxcy. They sought sleeping quarters elsewhere on Deep Creek. However, in spite of her poor first efforts at cooking, both men agreed to board with the Tabors, and their money provided a steady income for the newlyweds. Horace broke the soil for planting, and whenever possible, Augusta joined him in the fields. In May 1857, she was obviously pregnant. Robbed of a flexible waistline, she had to devise new motions for her back and knees as she bent to her tasks of hoeing and weeding. The work was heavy. All water had to be carried by bucket from the creek. All waste materials had to be disposed of away from the house. Time and custom had decreed that these were women's spheres of operations, and Augusta forced her fragile frame to the task, determined to be the equal of her man in effort if not in fact.

Unfortunately, that first year was a time of drought. With no rain to nourish the crops, the harvest was inadequate. The Tabors' only income was the money that Sam and Nathaniel paid Augusta for their board. The need for capital was imperative with a baby on the way. Horace decided to put his masonry skills to use and took employment at Fort Riley, a government post about eighteen miles from home. Most of the buildings at the fort were fashioned from stone, so there was steady work for Horace. He stayed at the fort most of the week, coming home only for the short weekends. Augusta was haunted by fear that the baby would arrive while Horace was absent.

At this juncture, worry was a constant with Augusta. There was little money, the crops had failed, the baby was due, and she was alone on the open prairie. Indians were in the area, and Augusta, like most white people, feared them, although they appeared but seldom. The constant curse was snakes. Drought did not deter them; only winter interrupted their insidious invasion. Augusta loved animals, but those she was accustomed to were warm and responsive to the human touch. These snakes were repulsive, cold, and sinister. Unable to look them in

Augusta Tabor as a young
woman. *Laforgue Private
Collection.*

the eye, she deemed them the most untrustworthy of God's creatures.
They sought out the shade in Augusta's house. Silently, stealthily,
they slithered across the floor. They hid themselves under her bed or
secreted themselves on the shelves where she kept her pails and pipkins.
If fright could be fatal, they would have been the death of her.

In October 1857, as Augusta writes with maddening lack of detail,
"baby came" to live with them. Nathaniel Maxcy must have made
some heroic effort in this vital production because both parents were
in complete agreement in naming their firstborn Nathaniel Maxcy
Tabor. If Horace were away at Fort Riley, as he should have been,
Nathaniel either delivered the baby himself or took Augusta into
Manhattan, the nearest town, where she could have had the help of
a doctor. Their son was always called Maxcy, possibly to prevent
confusion with his namesake.

During the winter, when snow and cold curtailed outside activities,
Augusta perfected her management of the No. 7 cookstove, learning
how to regulate the heat, adjust the damper, and bank the logs so
that there would be sufficient embers in the morning to stoke a new
fire. Winter was usually the time for mending and sewing, and with

the baby growing every day, she needed a variety of garments to keep him comfortable.

Undaunted by their first year's crop failure, the Tabors set about seeding once again in spring 1858. They added a cow and some chickens to the farm, and these were Augusta's special charges. She also adopted a mongrel dog whom she affectionately named "Petty." He was company for her while Horace was absent, and he worried the snakes so that they rarely surprised her anymore.

Summer 1858 proved better for farming. The rains were adequate and the harvest was plentiful. All their neighbors profited from these blessings, however, and the law of supply and demand established low prices due to the overabundance of crops. In order to make any profit on their corn, Augusta had to shell each ear. The Tabors bundled the shelled corn into a wagon and hauled it to Fort Riley, where the market and price were better. However, it took two days for the complete circuit, and the Tabors soon realized that the effort was not commensurate with the return.

That winter, Augusta convinced Horace that they needed a new and better house to accommodate their larger family. Horace undertook to make a stone house with a small upstairs bedroom. This building would have provided a more spacious and secure dwelling for the Tabors, but they never got around to living in it. Early in 1859, about the time they should have moved into the new quarters, they heard rumors about gold discoveries farther west in what was then known as the Pike's Peak region of Kansas Territory. Horace was intrigued. In Vermont, he had become convinced that hard work was not the answer to accumulating wealth. No matter how hard they had labored, the Tabors had never had enough. As a gamester, Horace also knew that money won was far sweeter than money earned by the sweat of furrowed brow. He wanted his turn at life's golden gambling tables. They decided to head for the Rocky Mountains.

Moving west meant that the Tabors would have to sell or mortgage the Zeandale property. In exchange for $150 cash, they mortgaged the 160 acres to William Shepard. Now appeared another discrimination for married women. Augusta's name never appeared on the patents for the Kansas property. As was his right, Horace held the acreage in his

Nathaniel Maxcy Tabor, the only child of Horace and Augusta, seen here as a teenager. *Colorado Historical Society.*

name only. However, when the mortgage was signed, Augusta's name was joined with that of her husband. Together they promised to repay the $150 with interest at 2½ percent per month. Repayment was due in a year's time. Although title to property was not shared, debts and liens were assigned to both. This practice caused one pioneer woman, who had been saddled with bills owed by her deceased husband, to complain, "When those obligations were made, I was my husband's silent partner — a legal nonentity — with no voice or power for self-protection under the sun, but when penalty accrued, I was his legal representative." When a similar situation forced her mother into a debtor's role, Susan B. Anthony decided to become a crusader for women's rights.

Knowing the dangers and uncertainties that would be part of migrating further into the unsettled West, Horace suggested to Augusta that she return to Maine and stay with her family until he had established a career in some mining camp. Augusta vehemently refused. She had married him until death did them part, and she intended to do her share always, no matter where he went or what work he undertook. In considering the whole adventure, Horace realized that if Augusta came along, then Samuel and Nathaniel would very likely accompany them, and their board money would be a stable income as it had been in the past. To augment the $150 they received for the mortgage on the farm, Horace returned to Fort Riley and saved his wages until they were ready to leave for the shining prospects of gold camps in the Rocky Mountain West.

Horace Tabor as a young man.
Laforgue Private Collection.

III
To Denver and Beyond

O n the fifth day of May in 1859, Horace, Augusta, and Maxcy, accompanied by Sam Kellogg and Nathaniel Maxcy, left the security of Zeandale for the little-known and inadequately chartered West. In the wagon they took water and a few months supply of food and necessaries. Tied to the rear of the wagon were their cows and several young steers. Petty the dog rode most of the time with Augusta in the rear of the wagon.

There were as yet few well-marked trails to the Rocky Mountains. Two general routes were possible: the more southerly Smoky Hill Trail, which was shorter, and the more northerly Republican Route, which was longer. The Republican Route was better defined since it carried regular traffic between Fort Riley and Fort Kearney in Nebraska Territory. That was reason enough for the Tabors to choose the Republican Route. Horace Greeley, who had traversed the road only a month later than the Tabors, reported that the country around the Republican was the acme of barrenness and desolation. According to him, there

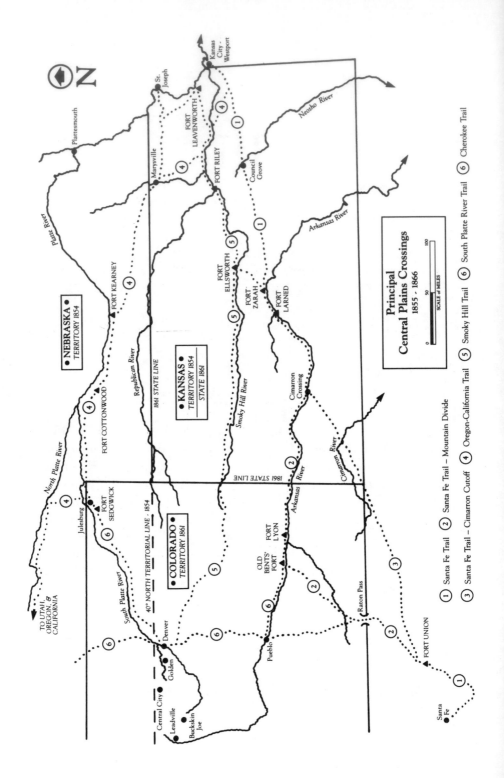

Principal
Central Plains Crossings
1855 - 1866

SCALE of MILES
0   50   100

① Santa Fe Trail ② Santa Fe Trail – Mountain Divide
③ Santa Fe Trail – Cimarron Cutoff ④ Oregon-California Trail ⑤ Smoky Hill Trail ⑥ South Platte River Trail ⑥ Cherokee Trail

were only a few scrubby cottonwood trees; the grass was meager and poor. The soil was excessively alkaline and supported nothing but a tangle of intermittent grassroots. Near the few watering places, sand was deep and treacherous. Once on the road, however, there was no turning back for the Tabors.

The trip to the Rocky Mountains was even more difficult for Augusta than the two-week trek from Westport to Zeandale had been. Her normal chores increased with the care and attention needed for her year-old son, who was fretful from teething. More animals in tow also demanded her ministrations. Farmwork, however, had inured Augusta to the stress and discomfort of manual labor. By this time she had resigned herself to the absence of women, and she had adjusted to the more brusque and outspoken manner of men. Even though she was suffering from fever and ague, and weighed but ninety pounds, she faithfully performed her domestic duties and lent a hand to the men when the wagon bogged down in the ruts and underbrush.

Riding in the wagon was itself no joy. The "road" was nothing more than a cattle path with barely visible tracks. Sometimes it was a relief to walk beside the wagon instead of being jolted inside it. Cooking chores were as constant as hunger and frequently as irritating. Back in Zeandale, Augusta had conquered the idiosyncracies of the No. 7 iron stove. Now she had to learn how to make a fire on the move, using buffalo chips as fuel. Whenever they stopped for meals, it was her task to walk over the land (sometimes searching for miles), picking up whatever droppings she could find. Once ignited, the chips burned well, but if the wind blew (and it generally did), the fire would blow every which way, and she would have to scoop up the glowing embers and return them to the central fire. Sometimes she did this three or four times before she could thoroughly heat whatever she was preparing. The smoke also bothered her eyes and lungs. Sweating over a hot stove was recreation compared to this type of outdoor cooking.

Indians appeared frequently along the route. The open prairie had for centuries been their land, and in spite of treaties and promises from the government, they considered this rolling country their private hunting ground. On the whole, the Indians were friendly, since the gold rush was in its infancy and the hordes of hopefuls had not yet begun to trespass and kill off the buffalo herds. The migrants knew so little about the Indians that fear compelled them to hate those whom they did not understand. In Zeandale, Augusta had heard her neighbors talking about Indians, but she had no first-hand knowledge of them and was uncertain how to accept those they met as they traveled through the open spaces.

In spring 1859, there were already some disillusioned gold seekers returning empty-handed to the East. They had tried to find Eldorado and failed, their high hopes shot down by leaden reality. They warned the Tabors of the dangers and disappointments ahead. "It's all a hoax," they said. "Go back!" Horace, however, was sure that this time fate had dealt him a straight flush, and he refused to throw in his hand. But for Augusta, it was sobering to come across skeletal remains bleaching on the ground. Her heart ached with doubt when she saw mounds of heaped-up dirt upon which some sorrowing father or brother had raised a wooden cross. She would clutch her son tightly in her arms, determined to protect him from whatever evil lurked in this formidable land. After all, they had come west to find a brighter future for their baby, not a bleaker one.

Every Sunday they had an unvarying routine. The men would leave with their guns soon after breakfast, hoping to kill enough game to last the week. Augusta would clean up the breakfast dishes and then wash all the soiled clothing that had accumulated. Indians made her task more difficult. They thought it sport to wallow in the very streams where she was trying to clean the clothes, and they roiled the waters unnecessarily. The braves stayed close by her, observing everything she did. They begged for bits of food as she prepared bread and meat for the coming week. Augusta was particularly repulsed by the way the Indians sat on their haunches, picking lice from their heads and cracking the vermin between their fingernails, then biting them with their teeth.

When the men returned from the hunt, they rested while Augusta, who had been busy all day, too, prepared the evening meal. After dinner, while the hunters skinned their kill, the group talked about the events of the day and enjoyed the warmth and friendly glow of the campfire. Finally, they rounded up the cattle before bedding down for the night.

Six weeks after they left Zeandale, the voyagers arrived in sight of the Rocky Mountains. The scene was awesome and inspiring. Augusta forgot her weariness. She gloried in the spectacle of majestic mountains with their lofty peaks rising proudly above the peasant plains, and their crests crowned with a diadem of snow. During the third week of June in 1859, the Tabors arrived in Denver. They were part of a very special group — the fifty-niners.

The Tabors, Samuel Kellogg, and Nathaniel Maxcy camped along the Platte River in Denver where the railroad yards are now located. The cattle were so footsore and weary they had to rest; so the party remained in the city until the first of July. The travelers looked about the town and found it a crude city whose several streets boasted a dozen or more buildings. There were cabins on roughly laid-out thoroughfares. In among the structures were tents of several Indian tribes, mostly Arapaho and Cheyenne. Bewhiskered miners were panning for gold right along the banks of nearby Cherry Creek. Augusta estimated that she was the eleventh woman to arrive in this frontier

Denver City, then part of Kansas Territory, as it looked about the time the Tabors arrived. *Frank Leslie's Magazine.*

An artist's depiction of a campsite in Denver, the goal of the Tabors when they left their farm in Kansas. *Frank Leslie's Magazine.*

outpost. Although there were probably at least three dozen women who entered Denver before her, even those figures attest that women were rare specimens in the developing West.

Horace, Sam, and Nathaniel gathered all the information they could about the location of the best gold strikes. They decided to test their luck in the Gregory Diggings, where John Gregory had found gold in paying quantities in the mountains about forty miles northwest of Denver.

On the first of July, the argonauts headed up into the foothills. The Rocky Mountains had been aptly named, and the terrain was especially difficult for people who had lived for several years on the flat Kansas prairie. Following Clear Creek, these eager fifty-niners arrived at the place where Golden now stands. From this valley, they could see the steep inclines of the nearby mountains. Horace decided the men could make better time by themselves on foot. They left Augusta with the baby and cattle in an improvised camp, took their provisions on their backs, and set out to reconnoiter. Augusta was once again on her own resources in strange surroundings. She had no idea of the limits of these formidable foothills. What danger was hidden behind the horizon? Were bears and predatory animals lurking in the shadows of the rocks and fir trees? Was that noise the sighing of the wind or a signal to marauding Indian bands?

During the day, the anxiety was bearable. Augusta was busy rounding up the cattle and tending her baby. Daylight gave her the advantage of sight; blind night made her vulnerable to the terrors of her own vivid imagination. Thoughts of her Maine home and the protection of her warm family circle increased the pain of her loneliness. For three long weeks she kept to this bleak and solitary camp life with only the faithful Petty to reassure her.

On the twenty-sixth of July, the exploring trio returned hallooing as they descended the mountains. They were satisfied with prospects at the Gregory Diggings, and they wanted to move on. Picking up again and gathering the oxen and cows, the hopefuls took off on the next step of their adventure. The ascent was strenuous. Once again, there was no road, only the suggestion of a trail. Because of the width of the wagon, they had to stop and widen the path, chopping down trees, flattening shrubs, and moving rocks. On the steepest inclines, they had to empty the wagon to ease the load for the oxen. Then each person shouldered the paraphernalia and trudged to a higher point where they restacked the items into the wagon.

Hills go up, but they also go down. On sharp declines, the travelers learned how to make an effective brake by tying a tree to the back of the wagon. Frequently, when they stopped for the night, the mountainside was so steep that they could not lie down flat. They drove stakes into the ground and rolled a log against them. Bracing their feet against this, the weary travelers slept in an almost upright position. In spite of the difficulties, Augusta loved sleeping outdoors, delighting in the star-strewn heavens and the clear, sweet-smelling atmosphere.

It was evidently just what her frail body needed, because as the months went by, she grew ever stronger. Nature was bountiful, and Augusta enriched herself with these gifts so freely given. Her body grew strong as her spirit soared.

They spent three weeks hacking their way into the gold camp called Russell's Gulch. Here Augusta enjoyed a pleasant respite. At this newly formed settlement, she came across another woman, Mary York. The exclusive male companionship never filled Augusta's need for small talk, and she and Mary spent hours exchanging stories of their past joys and present woes. With empathy and sensitivity, Augusta listened to the tragic tale that Mary had to tell.

Mary York had been born near Windsor Castle, London, in 1830. She was, therefore, the same age as Horace. She had parents who were enthusiastically Irish and abhorred the fact that one of their children had been born on English soil. When Mary was twelve years old, her parents took her to Canada, along with an older brother. The father died en route and was buried at sea. His heartbroken widow survived only three months longer.

The orphan children were separated and taken care of by different families. Mary became the servant of a Canadian household, but she was very unhappy in this position, carefully saved her money, and eventually set out on her own.

She traveled by herself to Baltimore, Maryland, and entered the employ of a family named McGee. These people wanted very much to go West and promised to take Mary with them. The three set out on what appeared to be a congenial trip. The wife was especially kind, but the character of the man changed. Overhearing an argument between the couple, Mary discovered that the reason McGee wanted to take her with them was to use her for immoral purposes in the fledgling towns where men willingly paid for female companionship. Mrs. McGee violently objected to the scheme, but to no avail. Mary contemplated suicide. One day when they stopped to prepare lunch, Mary went down to the stream for water and hid there among the willows. If the McGees came looking for her, she intended to drown herself.

As she waited in great sorrow at the edge of the water, contemplating her sad situation, a stranger appeared. He introduced himself as Green Russell and told Mary that he was returning to the Rocky Mountains with a group of friends from Georgia. He assured her of his protection if she would accompany them. Mary trusted him, believing he was a guardian angel come as an answer to her prayers. At the Gregory Diggings and nearby Russell Gulch, Mary settled into her fate. She cooked for the miners and washed their clothes. "But I was not raised for this common labor," she protested.

How well Augusta could empathize! These two understood the special sorrows of frontier women and the unusual difficulties under which they lived. As pioneers, they shared a unique bond. They were among the first to tread new paths, testing untried territory. They knew personally, painfully, the lacerating labor from which this new land was born.

Mary York would eventually become the wife of a famous sheriff of Central City, William Cozens. They were the first couple to be married by Father (later Bishop) Joseph P. Machebeuf in territory that would soon become the State of Colorado.

Augusta disliked leaving her new-found friend, but Horace and his partners were anxious to get on and start their gold panning. They pushed on to a location called Payne's Bar (now known as Idaho Springs). Here the miners greeted Augusta with warmth and appreciation. She was the first woman to arrive in camp. For them, Augusta was a poignant reminder of the mother they respected, the wife they hungered for, the sister they remembered. Collectively, the homesick migrants cut trees, laid them up four feet in height, and fashioned a house for her, using her own seven- by nine-foot tent for a roof.

While Horace, Sam, and Nathaniel went a few miles farther west to Spanish Bar (near the present Stanley Mines) to pan for gold every day, Augusta established a routine that she repeated in every gold camp they moved to. She opened a bakery to sell pies and bread. She also boarded as many men as she could accommodate at her table. She sold milk to the settlers and made butter for them to buy. She was overly busy from morning to night but felt content that she was able to add so much steady income to the gold dust that Horace washed out of South Clear Creek.

Gold Rush miners. Note the sluice boxes that these men are using to work a placer mine. *Denver Public Library, Western History Department.*

At Payne's Bar, Augusta perfected another talent — the art of healing. Nathaniel Maxcy came down with what was called "Mountain Fever" — a combination of high temperature, dysentery, and chills. Along with her other duties, Augusta nursed him back to health. She placed him outside in the wagon to reduce contagion for the family. There she gave the patient the attention he needed both as physician and nurse. When the miners saw how effective her ministrations were, she was soon in demand for all kinds of complaints, especially gunshot wounds. In the mining towns, tempers were as short as women; too often violence settled an argument.

For many reasons, Augusta was a favorite with the miners. They treated her with respect and consideration. One of the people who gave her a helping hand in that year of 1859 was the father of Lewis C. Gandy, author of *The Tabors: A Footnote of Western History*. In return for his meals, the senior Gandy chopped wood for Augusta, carried water, washed dishes, and milked her cow.

Toward the end of September, the first snow came. An old miner approached Horace and warned him about the danger of snowslides and avalanches. He convinced Horace that Payne's Bar was no safe place for a woman and child. Taking the prospector's advice, the anxious Horace packed their belongings into the wagon and set off for Denver and the comparative safety of city living.

In Denver, the Tabors took up residence in a room over Vasquez's store on what was then called Ferry Street. It was not much of a dwelling. Due to the slanted roof, there was little standing room, and the wooden floor was very rough. It was, however, the first real building that Augusta had lived in since leaving Kansas. At a rent of twenty-five dollars a month, Augusta worried about the cost. She had learned never to spend a dime where a nickel would do.

Thanks to hard work, especially with the cooking and other services that Augusta provided, the Tabors counted their first summer in the Rocky Mountains a success. They had actually accumulated enough money to pay off the farm in Kansas and provide for their keep through the coming winter. They made the acquaintance of a young man (whom Augusta fails to name in her diary) who was returning to the East. They entrusted him with the money for the farm and also with Augusta's precious dog Petty. She considered the upkeep for her pet and felt that as much as she loved him, his rations would be too expensive for a struggling family.

With Augusta settled in the room at the Vasquez store, where she continued to set table for paying customers, Horace returned to his prospecting hole at Payne's Bar. There he found that his claim had been jumped by the very miner who had advised him to go down to Denver. Claim jumping was a studied art in those days before the newcomers had time to enact laws protecting their business interests. It was all too easy for a sharper to take advantage of a greenhorn. Horace learned from this experience and never made that mistake again.

With his claim gone and time on his hands, Horace went to Colorado City (near present Colorado Springs), where he put up one of the first buildings in the area. He was convinced along with many others that this centrally located town would soon become the state capital, but after seven legislative sessions, the capital was finally established in Denver. According to historian Leroy Hafen (seriously, or with tongue in cheek), this decision was made because Denver was the only city that had enough women to feed and lodge the legislators.

In winter 1859, Horace returned to Denver. He was happy to be reunited with Augusta and baby Maxcy, and they made plans to move their belongings south to Colorado City. Denver, however, was humming with rumors about a sizable gold find in South Park, and the lure of easy good fortune was irresistible to Horace. He readily gave up his plans for town promotion to renew his role as a seeker after gold. As soon as the weather permitted, the Tabors intended to set out for the high mountain passes and test the Arkansas River for whatever riches it might carry. The Tabors were persistent and prepared to stay in the territory until it yielded their hearts' desire.

IV
From Denver to the High Country

Rumors about the gold strike in South Park created a lodestone for wealth seekers living in Denver. During the winter, a group of about two dozen prospectors made plans to head for the high country; the Tabors were among them. Unfortunately at this very time, Augusta was stricken with illness, but some of the men would brook no delay and took off by themselves. In a matter of days, Augusta was carried from her sick bed into the wagon, and the remaining prospectors decamped for the high country on February 14, 1860. On this expedition, the Tabors were in the company of four men. Two were the familiar Sam Kellogg and Nathaniel Maxcy. In her diary, Augusta refers to the others as "Mac" and "Glover."

Their first stop was Montana City, a rude settlement of about twenty cabins located a mile south of Denver. Most of the buildings were deserted. The Tabor party went into one and spent the night there. The cabin had no floor, no window, no door. Augusta slept on the bare ground that night but admitted that she awoke refreshed and

Blake Street in Denver in 1860, the year the Tabors left to find gold in the Arkansas Valley. *Colorado Historical Society.*

feeling better than she had in Denver. Seemingly, she thrived on adversity.

Because of Augusta's weakened condition, the four men helped with the cooking chores until her vitality returned. One night these venturers camped on the banks of Plum Creek. From there, they continued south. As they passed through Colorado City, the town organizers gave Augusta several free lots simply because she was a woman and the wife of one of their foremost boosters. After four days of travel from Denver, the Tabors arrived at Manitou Springs. Unfamiliar with the properties of mountain spring water, Augusta stirred up a batch of biscuits, but they turned yellow and tasted so strongly of soda that the men did not relish them, in spite of their huge appetites. To pioneers on the trail, however, quality was never so important as quantity. Their hunger would tolerate badly cooked, poorly seasoned, and severely scorched food just so long as there was enough of it. They ate anything placed before them, tasty or not.

The Tabors remained in the Manitou area for a week. Horace and his friends hired out as road builders on the trail leading over Ute Pass. They did this not only to earn money, but also to facilitate their own ascent into the mountains. Once they were beyond the established roadway, the going was very slow. They forged their way, a wheel revolution at a time. So far as they knew, they were the pathmakers on this route into South Park.

It took two weeks for the wagon to make it into the park. The weather had been changeable, including some snow squalls. The wet roads did not make the travel any faster or easier. The weeks of sickness had taken their toll on Augusta, and the exertions of the climb kept her in constant pain. In spite of this, when she looked upon the beauties of South Park, she became enraptured. The scene was picture perfect, as if straight from the hand of God. The park looked like a cultivated field, with herds of deer and antelope grazing in utmost freedom and tranquility. All this set against the sublime backdrop of Weston Pass. Augusta felt that she was looking on Paradise reborn.

As the wagon lumbered slowly into the wide landscape, the travelers decided to camp on the banks of what was then called Jefferson Creek. The men went upstream to look for fish and test the streambed for gold. Augusta knelt by the creek to wash the soiled clothing of this party of seven. The water was icy cold, but there were many rocks upon which to pound the clothes and make them clean. The swift-running creek quickly carried the filth downstream. The Tabors stayed in the park several days, trying to locate the party of men who had set out from Denver shortly before them. Those men had traveled by way of Kenosha Pass, but they had expected to rendezvous somewhere in the park.

As the Tabors traveled through South Park, they came to Salt Creek late one night. They first tested the water, remembering the bitter experience they had had in Manitou. The creek was very saline, and neither they nor the cattle could slake their thirst. They went to bed without water and with growing hunger. Their supplies were rapidly diminishing. The night was cold, and they had many reasons to feel discouraged and disheartened.

Horace and Augusta were sleeping in their tent when a donkey, emboldened by the cold, came right toward the tent. He walked straight into their small fire and stood there until his fetlocks became singed. The odor was sickening. But Augusta felt sorry for the shivering animal. She rubbed down his bedraggled coat and wiped the frost from his ears and muzzle. The jack responded to her kindness and served Augusta well in the weeks to come.

Next day the Tabors camped on Trout Creek. The men decided to go singly in search of the first party. Each taking a gun, they set out north, south, east, and west. The man who located their friends was to shoot into the air as a signal to the others. In unknown and forbidding territory, Augusta was once again a solitary sentinel. She and the baby shared the open wilderness. She regretted having sent her faithful dog back to Kansas. He would have been some comfort and reassurance. To take his place, however, was the donkey. As if sensitive to her mood, it pushed its way into the tent and lay down near her and the baby. Augusta put her head on the rough coat and wept out her fear and loneliness. The men were much later than expected in returning to camp, but she kept a small fire going outside the tent. Using that for direction, the explorers came back about midnight. They had not located their fellow travelers.

Uncertain which direction to follow, the men opted next day to follow the Arkansas River, hoping to find a safe place to cross to the other side. The river ran rapidly, fed by melting snows. Boulders jutting upward through the current were outlined with ice. The men tested every few feet to locate a safe place to ford the stream. When they decided on a likely spot, they drove the cattle in. After their long upward climb, the oxen were thin, weak, and tired. The freezing water turned them into statues. They refused to move. Finally, the men had no alternative but to plunge into the stream themselves, rope the animals, and drag them across. The faithful little donkey took care of Augusta and the baby, ferrying them safely across, even though nothing but his nose rose above the boisterous waters.

With all the problems, it took them six hours to ford the Arkansas River. Then Horace and the others built a fire to dry out their clothing and warm the cattle. The oxen were indispensable to the quest and not one could be spared. The supplies of the travelers were almost exhausted. Soon they would be forced to eat the animals in order to avoid starvation. To let the cattle recuperate, the party stayed about one week in this camp. Every day each man would set out — one to hunt, one to fish, one or more to pan for gold. The few specks of gold they collected kept their hopes high and made the difficulties fade into insignificance. At night they would play cards by the campfire and talk about home and the comforts they had left behind. Always they assured each other that tomorrow would be a better day.

Still following the river, the gold seekers eventually camped where Cache Creek empties into the Arkansas. Here they decided to make a real attempt at gold mining. Horace and Nathaniel whipsawed some boards and shaped them into sluice boxes; then they cut riffles from a log, made a ditch from the creek, and began washing the bank away. Every night they collected plenty of fine gold from the riffles. The gold, however, was trapped within black sand and they could not free it. Finally, they resorted to the very slow process of culling the sands with a magnet. This tedious job fell to Augusta. After her day's chores of washing and cooking, caring for the cattle, and soothing the baby, she would finecomb the sands, trying to free the elusive gold. For hours of such exacting work, she would garner only a pennyworth of the precious metal.

Because their provisions were at a dangerous low, the guns and fish hooks of the men supplied most of their food. Augusta was ashamed of the monotonous fare. With only venison, mountain sheep, and fish for staples, she varied the menu by the method of cooking — broiled for breakfast, fried for lunch, and boiled for supper.

After working the creek bed for about a month, the outlook grew dismal, and an air of despondency developed in camp. Then suddenly, a stranger appeared out of the wilderness. He came toward them astride a donkey. The rider had seen their campfire and came to investigate. His greatest surprise was seeing a woman in these rugged mountains. Augusta was the first woman he had seen since leaving civilization. The stranger advised them to move upstream about twenty miles, then cross the river again. Here they would find a gold-producing gulch — California Gulch — from which he had just come. Gold in that location, he told them, was coarser than the fine stuff the Tabors were collecting in their sluice boxes. Then he showed them some nuggets he had taken from the diggings. Hope grew with desire, and the Tabors determined to follow his directions. Wealth might soon be theirs.

The very next morning, the eager travelers broke camp. When they finally spotted the bald mountain that the stranger had told them about, they decided to cross the river directly, because at this point the bed seemed broad and shallow. The men drove the cattle into the water, leaving Augusta and the baby inside the wagon. As they neared the opposite bank of the river, the wagon fell into a deep channel. The bed rose above the wheels and started to float downstream, taking Augusta with it, the child clutched tightly in her arms.

As the wagon rapidly filled with water, Augusta panicked. Had she come so far to die so soon? She searched desperately for help. Noticing willow branches hanging over the bank, she reached frantically for their support, the child still cradled in one arm. When she grasped the willows, she clung to them with every reserve of strength she could muster. Two of the men scrambled onto the bank, reached out to save her and her precious burden, and hauled them to shore. Safely on dry land, Augusta relaxed and lapsed into unconsciousness.

How the men rescued the wagon and reorganized the load, she never knew. She did not revive from her ordeal until the wagon was actually at the mouth of California Gulch. Here they arrived at what they hoped would be the promised golden land on May 8, 1860, having endured all kinds of travail on the way. It had taken them three long, exhausting months to travel from Denver into this rough mountain camp.

Once more, Augusta was the first woman to arrive. The men were so impressed and so delighted with her presence that they started making a cabin for her. With all the miners exerting their combined efforts, they completed a twelve-by-fourteen-foot cabin by nightfall. Augusta was so pleased with their admiration and concern! She felt like a princess coming into her kingdom at last. The prospectors had been without adequate rations for many days, and the Tabors now slaughtered their oxen to share their food with the community.

Repeating her successful enterprises at Payne's Bar and Denver City, Augusta's housewifely skills filled needs that the miners were willing to pay and pay well for. She immediately began to set table for many boarders, even though her larder was all but empty. Since she had achieved a mastery of culinary techniques, she was able to adjust and alter recipes, substituting a pat of caring and a handful of make-do for tablespoons of this and cups of that.

The gold returns in California Gulch were so good that the Tabors felt they had arrived at a permanent location. Horace dismantled their wagon to fashion tables and stools, but they were so busy all day long and far into the night that they really had little need for the chairs because there was no time to sit down and relax. Augusta stayed on her feet from daybreak until long after sunset.

The cry of "gold!" went down from the mountaintops far out to the plains, even to the coastal lands. Soon came an army of people marching into this narrow gulch. Augusta, if cloned, could have run a chain of restaurants. She boarded as many men as she could, laundered as many clothes as her washtub could immerse, and still found time to handle the duties of mail clerk. The post office was set up in a corner of the Tabor cabin. As Augusta herself admitted, few women would have tolerated the constant, tobacco-chewing, crusty crowd that the mailcall drew. The Tabors owned the only gold scales in the gulch, and after the regular cares of the day, Augusta patiently weighed out the dust that each and every miner brought to her house.

As the end of the summer season in California Gulch, the Tabors had accumulated $4,000 from their combined efforts. It was an impressive sum, more than they had made in the first years of their marriage from backbreaking farmwork.

Even so, one of the first arguments between Augusta and Horace developed at this time. A man by the name of William Van Brooklyn was the mail express carrier. He wanted Augusta to board him in exchange for his claim on the gulch. Augusta did not like the man, however. He was basically lazy (a trait the energetic Augusta despised), and he may have had other characteristics distasteful to a sensitive woman. She refused to include him among the many boarders she willingly handled. Later, when his claim proved to be worth $80,000, Horace reminded Augusta that they could have been rich much sooner if she had accepted Van Brooklyn's offer.

Meanwhile, Horace, always a congenial and popular man, entered into the politics of the mining camp, using the skills he had learned in the Topeka legislature. When the prospectors decided that they must have some form of government and law to safeguard their mining claims, they made a motion to establish the Territory of Jefferson. All mining districts were eligible to vote on this proposition. From California Gulch, the miners chose Horace as their representative to the constitutional convention which was scheduled to be held in Denver.

As winter began to approach in September, Augusta took Maxcy and headed for the Pierce home in Maine. On the way, she stopped off in Zeandale to visit her former neighbors and proudly purchase an additional 160 acres of farmland adjoining their original homestead. Although she had helped to pay for both patents, only Horace's name appears on the deeds. This was perfectly legal but certainly not equitable.

Of the $4,000 which the Tabors had earned through their common effort, Horace had given Augusta $1,000 for the trip east. Ever conscious of each penny, Augusta made a detailed account of how she spent the money. She paid $400 for the quarter section of land in Kansas. She allotted $200 for her traveling expenses to Maine. To supplement that, she acted as cook for the wagon train that carried her eastward. At home, her family generously replenished her wardrobe. (She confessed in her diary that she had not spent a single penny on clothing since her wedding day.)

When Horace joined Augusta in Maine later in the year, their combined tales of the far West, heightened by Horace's explicit account of fortunes easily made, aroused the interest of Augusta's brothers and sisters. They listened eagerly to everything these two fifty-niners had to recount. Weighing the balance of difficulties with opportunities, brother Frank and sister Lilly decided to accompany the Tabors when they retraced their route to California Gulch in the spring.

This time on the way west, Horace and Augusta bought supplies to take to the mining camp, using the final $400 of the $1,000 which Horace had allotted for the trip home. Having experienced the vagaries of camp life, Horace realized that acting as a sutler to supply the needs of prospectors provided a steadier income than mining itself. He would

An artist's depiction of a played-out gulch after the miners had left. *Harper's Weekly, November 27, 1875.*

continue to look for the elusive gold and bought many mining properties, but it was obvious that he could make good money in merchandising, especially since Augusta was available to keep the store going while he continued to work his mining interests.

On April 12, 1861, while the Tabor party was in St. Joseph, Missouri, the first guns fired at Fort Sumter signaled the start of the Civil War. By this time, Horace, thirty years of age, was not interested in enlisting in the army. He considered that he had already done his share for abolition with his work in Kansas. The issue of the Civil War centered around slavery. The struggle to emancipate blacks and later to grant them the privileges of full citizenship was of especial interest to women. To some degree, their own cause for the franchise had become inextricably involved with the blacks' right to vote. As blacks had been refused the franchise because of the color of their skin, women protested that they had been denied this right because of their sex.

It took the Tabors six weeks to travel from Maine to the land that

Congress created as Colorado Territory in February 1861. The weather, as it frequently is in springtime, proved very unpredictable. Sun, snow, rain, and hail were all possible, even in the course of a single day.

When the Tabors reached South Park, it was around the first week of May, and a heavy, wet snowstorm covered the countryside. Their path led over the slopes of the Mosquito Range. At that time the route was called the California Gulch Road and today is known as Weston Pass. As they neared their goal, the entire complement, male and female, shoveled their way. As they neared their destination, California Gulch, the inhabitants started digging out of the camp to meet the travelers. The Tabors were the first group in a week to enter the camp, which had been shut off because of the storm.

The local hotel gave the newcomers a warm welcome. Supper consisted of beef, bread, and dried applesauce, but it was served with such a genuine glow of friendship that the Tabors accepted it as a banquet. The miners and their newly arrived guests celebrated with a night of dancing and festivity. These early settlers played as hard as they worked; it was necessary for sane survival. The fiddlers kept the dancing feet in tune all through the night. There were gambling and cards for the men, conversation for the women. The Tabors rejoiced at being home, but they were not destined to remain in that location for long.

Note: On the second floor of the Tabor house in Leadville, there is an old trunk which Peggy DuCharme says shows water marks. Could it be the one that survived the dunking in the Arkansas River?

V
The Years at
Buckskin Joe

Prospectors were a restless crew. They were ready at the fading of the color to pick up pans and sluice boxes and move on to wherever the golden nuggets shone again. By 1861, the metal had run its course in the streams of California Gulch, but over the pass, a man named Phillips had discovered a lode in the town called Buckskin Joe.

This town was situated across the divide from California Gulch. It had been founded by a man named Joe Higginbottom, who had a penchant for fringed clothing made of animal skins — hence the town's name. Historians say it had been officially known as Laurette in honor of Laura and Jeanette, wives of two of the early comers, the Dodge brothers.

The Phillips lode promised to be a bonanza, and the influx of people to Buckskin Joe simulated a stampede. It was amazing how fast towns grew in those days. What for centuries had been virgin forest, unbeknownst to all but animals and a few transient Indian tribes, almost overnight became a place of habitation, with log cabins, tents, and a

Buckskin Joe in 1864, three years after the Tabors moved their store there. *Colorado Historical Society.*

few roughly outlined streets. Hotels were a must and saloons were of primary consideration. There was always a place designated for the stagecoaches to deposit the incoming wealth seekers. The inhabitants also needed cemeteries to bury the frequent victims of disease and the more numerous victims of violence.

In August 1861, the Tabors packed up their groceries, merchandise, and household equipment. With four-year-old Maxcy and Augusta's sister and brother, the family headed over the high range. If Horace were not lucky with his mining claims, Augusta knew that their sutler's store and her cooking and washing would make them more than self-sufficient.

At the top of the pass, a swirling, blinding snowstorm overtook the party. Unable to reach the toll gate where they knew there was a modest shelter for the man who collected the toll, the Tabors were forced to stop where they were and set up camp in the snow, which already measured three feet in depth. Spreading tarpaulins on top of the snow and covering themselves with every available blanket, the group slept well. In the morning, they found to their amazement that snow which they had kicked loose during the night had accumulated to a depth of several feet, and they found themselves deep into a snowbank where they were protected from the wind and weather. In fact, they felt so comfortable that they wanted to linger for a while under the covers. However, they needed to feed the cattle and prepare breakfast; so they were up and about as usual shortly after sunrise.

With its successful lodes producing close to a half million dollars in its first years, Buckskin Joe attracted some of Colorado's most famous characters. The Methodist minister, Reverend John Dyer, lived there, exhorting his flock on Sundays to embrace Christian virtues. During the week, he made his living by carrying mail back and forth over the high passes on hand-crafted skis. Father Joseph Machebeuf (who had officiated at the marriage of Mary York and William Cozens) took care of his scattered mountain congregations, arriving in a covered wagon which provided his living quarters, while the tailgate served as an outdoor altar when the Catholic faithful gathered for Sunday Mass.

Gold mining was becoming more sophisticated every year. Panning and sluicing were giving way to underground mining, which required more technical methods to bring out the ore and recover the gold from hard rock. One primitive way to separate the valuable metal was with a device known as an arrastra, a bowl-shaped, stone-lined depression in which heavy rocks were dragged round and round over the ore to crush it and free the gold. A horse, mule, or ox patiently circled the arrastra, providing the energy to haul the rocks. But even then, that crude technology was giving way to stamp mills. Buckskin Joe already boasted three such devices in which heavy iron blocks known as stamps were dropped on the ore to crush it and free the gold.

The Tabors remained in Buckskin Joe for seven years. Their store was the most successful in the area, and all the family bought heavily into nearby mines, going as far away as Tarryall to find paying, gold-producing sites. Horace had time now to become active in community politics. He was appointed roadmaster for an improved trail over Weston Pass. He therefore was a pathmaker in the most basic sense of the word. For six months he was superintendent of schools for Park County. What his philosophy of education was, one cannot say with certainty.

Ruins of the Tabors' store at Buckskin Joe. *Colorado Historical Society.*

He undoubtedly accepted the position for its community involvement and its access to political power and prestige. Belief in the value of education was Augusta's. When Horace wanted to put Maxcy to work in the store while he was still of school age, Augusta begged Horace to reconsider. She wanted their son to have the best education possible. Like all mothers, she had worked with him at home, teaching him letters and numbers. Now it was time for more formal education. She promised Horace that she would take on any extra work that needed to be done so that the boy would be free to continue his schooling.

Officially, Horace was the postmaster wherever the Tabors handled the mail. Under the law, only a husband could sign a contract. Although Augusta has frequently been referred to as the postmistress, she never legally held that position. As to who actually did the work, it is enlightening to read contemporary accounts.

The best picture of Horace and Augusta during their years at Buckskin Joe comes from the pen of Samuel Leach, who was postmaster at the nearby town of Sterling (sometimes known as Mosquito). He worked with the Tabors and knew them well. He wrote:

Saturday, October 25, 1862

Dear Brother George,
    Your welcome letter of the 7th instant reached me a few days since

as we now have two mails a week to Denver by way of Buckskin, or Buckskin Joe as they call it here. I have to go there twice a week and fetch the mail bags over to this camp as it is on the cards for me to be the postmaster here at Sterling and the petition has already gone into the Federal city, so I have to do the lugging. This change has come about in the last two weeks since I wrote you and I am relieved not to have to go four miles and back to Laurette, but only a mile back and forth to Buckskin where the mail for our camp is now delivered.

There is a postmistress at Buckskin and I shall tell you about her. She keeps a boarding house and runs a store much like the one I am in charge of here. Her husband works in the mines. They are a young couple about my own age, from down in Maine. He was a stone mason and worked for her father before they were married and during the time of their courtship he took up a homestead in Kansas. When they were married they went to Kansas to live and then crossed the plains and were in Denver, Idaho (Springs) and California Gulch for a while. He has made some money and has sent his wife back to Kansas to pay for the land there and to buy a 160 acre tract adjoining it and has made other investments. They are considered well to do here and they certainly are thrifty like the down eastern Yankees. She makes his shirts, puts new bosoms in the old ones, knits his socks, and makes her own soap. She is a good cook and the men like her pretty well although she is a driver.

Well, I spent four evenings there in the last two weeks helping her sort out the mail. Then we play seven-up and high-five for a while and she often takes a hand. I like these people very well. Their name is Tabor; her name is Augusta and his is Horace.

. . . Another letter to George:

March 10, 1863

. . . I passed last Sabbath with the Tabors. Their little boy is sitting up in his high chair to his meals and eats the same food as they do. He is large for his age and observing. His mother makes all his clothes and uses every flour, sugar and salt sack that comes into their possession to make underwear, panties and shirts for the boy. The Tabors are naturally thrifty, she more so perhaps than he is. In addition to tending store and looking after the mail she keeps boarders and makes a profit at it. They have accumulated about $20,000 in the time they have been in this territory and are planning to make a fortune here and return to the northeast to enjoy it in their old age.

Mr. Tabor said last Sabbath when we were talking of the future, "Sam, twenty years from now I shall have enough money to take things easy three months in each year and live comfortably at hotels in New York and Washington." His wife spoke up and said that she had no such thought but that they both ought to work and save as long as they were able to do so to make sure that they would be provided for in the lean years when they reached old age. She said he liked his leisure too well and did not exert himself as fully as he might do but took too much time off as it was for fishing, hunting and playing cards. She said he was too easy and if it were not for her looking out for him they would not have a dollar in the world. They got into an argument then and I . . . kept my mouth shut. But I like them both very much, each of them has fine qualities and they are good company.

Mrs. Tabor is going to plant a garden this spring, all vegetables. She had the seed sent her from Illinois. The ground is all cleared and spaded and well fertilized. She thinks in another month she will put in the seed — lettuce, carrots, onion sets, radishes, turnips, beets and potatoes. The men laugh at her and tell her the season is too short for her garden to grow and that the altitude is too high. She replies that she has read of vegetables being raised in the Alps and Apennines and that she can see no reason why they cannot be raised here. She had one hundred chickens sent up to her from Denver and has her own eggs. She also has a boar and a sow and a litter of little pigs. Her two cows keep her supplied with milk. She churns her own butter. I can see why he plans for three months in the year for vacation, for existence as it is now leaves no room for leisure. . . .

May 3, 1863

. . . It has spoiled me eating so often at the Tabors. I am becoming finicky.

Horace Tabor was here just now, stopping in on his way fishing to bring me a pot of beans his wife baked for me last night. I am looking forward to a hearty breakfast on them, baked with salt pork without molasses or other condiments to spoil them, they are just as I like them. I asked Mr. Tabor what he expected to catch as it was early for trout in the streams about here, and he said "nothing at all" — he was merely going for the sake of going fishing and laughed and went off in his lumbering fashion, pitching along in his high boots. He is very good-natured and full of fun and he has to take days off every now and then. . . .

I shall feast on my beans in the morning. They are real navy beans, too. Mrs. Tabor brought back a one hundred pound sack of them from the east last year. You cannot buy them around these parts: they are not in the market. She has her garden all planted, some from slips started in boxes in the house, and the rest put in the ground itself. You should see her place. Nothing slack or careless thereabouts, unless it is her husband. I cannot say that he does much himself, but he never makes fun of her, nor interferes at all and generally helps out when called upon, but he does not do anything on his own accord. As he says, he has to be prodded just like the ox they drove across the plains.

You would enjoy them; they are real Yankees and there is much to be learned from them. . . .

Leach's letters, verbatim, are extremely important. They are an eyewitness account from a disinterested contemporary. They are not biased in favor of either husband or wife. He likes them equally. He states that they were both generous and interesting personalities. He notes the attributes and defects of each of them. For Augusta he points out her determination and her drive and highlights the one characteristic that was frequently criticized — her sharp Maine tongue. Yet Horace's own admission that he had to be driven certainly explains how this trait may have been encouraged. As teamsters early discovered, some balky critters respond only to the prodding of the whip or the lash of well-honed words.

Another contemporary account mentions Augusta's sister Lilly.

Rupert M. Sherwood, who lived in Buckskin Joe in 1862 and who is remembered as the owner of Prunes, the hard-working burro, wrote in his biography that Buckskin Joe "was a live camp of a couple thousand miners and prospectors. H.A.W. Tabor had a grocery store and his wife Augusta and her sister ran a restaurant. It was a wild camp. We got our meals at Mrs. Tabor's restaurant." The food must have been delicious, prepared by an outstanding cook with fresh vegetables out of her well-tended garden.

At this juncture in their lives, the Tabors were successful both as entrepreneurs and as figures in the community. With Frank and especially Lilly living with them, Augusta must have been enjoying her life in the West.

During the years at Buckskin Joe, Augusta frequently helped Horace when he carried gold dust and nuggets down to the banks in Denver. Between the saddle blanket and the saddle, Augusta would place a sack containing the valuables. Robbery, of course, was a frequent highway happenstance. By concealing the gold beneath her, she ran little chance of detection. Thieves might rough up a man but they would hesitate in searching a woman.

Joseph Emerson Smith has left an account of the methods Augusta used in running a laundry for miners. Smith was a reporter for at least two Denver papers at different times during the 1880s and 1890s, and he was referred to as the "dean of newspapermen." During the summer months, Smith was a frequent visitor at the mountain home of Mrs. Elizabeth Entriken, an early pioneer and the sister of Reverend John Dyer, the snowshoeing minister of Park and Lake counties. Mrs. Entriken lived on property owned by her brother-in-law William Bailey, who had set up a camp stop (today, the town of Bailey) about midway between Denver and South Park.

According to Smith, one afternoon toward day's end in early summer 1865, a covered wagon with a weather-stained canvas top, drawn by two jaded mares, drew up alongside the stout log bridge that spanned the Platte River near Bailey's ranch. Mrs. Entriken, watching from the kitchen of her brother-in-law's hotel, was attracted by the brisk, purposeful manner of the husband and wife who were on board.

The man was well-built and vigorous. His wife was sunbonneted, her face framed by curly brown hair. While the man unharnessed and watered the horses, the woman removed pitch pine from the wagon and began shaping mounds of kindling on the ground. Then together, the couple set up several huge iron pots and suspended them over the piles of wood. The pots were filled with water from the stream and soon, steam was billowing into the open air.

From under the wagon seat, the woman removed a large square board. With a rock, she nailed it to the trunk of a spruce tree. Wagons were pulling in off the road, preparing to spend the night at Bailey's. The woman kept pointing to her sign as the teamsters rolled into the grove. Soon she had a crowd of men surrounding her. They were pulling off their shirts and handing them to her. Before long she had one kettle filled with the bubbling colors of checkered clothing.

Mrs. Entriken walked over to investigate. The sign stated boldly:

SHIRTS WASHED. 50 CENTS.

The sunbonneted woman came over to her and extended a hand wiped dry on her homespun apron.

"The name's Tabor," she told Mrs. Entriken. "This is the way I make money to help my husband. He's bent on prospecting and one of these days he'll make that big find. His luck will turn, just see if it won't! 'Til then I'm willing to do my part."

Soon the two women were comparing housekeeping notes, commiserating about the amount of lice the men carried on their clothing and the stench from personal items laundered too infrequently. Mrs. Entriken was accustomed to washing all the bed linens for the hotel. What she wanted to know from Augusta was how she could tell the shirts apart with so many being done at the same time.

"I put knotted strings in the tail. See?" and she gingerly picked up a blue flannel garment. From it dangled a white string with seven small knots. "On a bit of paper I put in pencil the man's name and give him a number. This man's got the figure '7', so I insert a string with that many knots on it."

As she watched the colored clothing writhing in the boiling water, Mrs. Entriken was in complete agreement as Augusta explained, "It's

49

worth four bits, what with getting out that dirt, then the boiling in clear water and the two rinsings, one hot, the other warm. I also sew on buttons and mend rips and tears."

Dreary as such a routine sounds, life at Buckskin Joe was not all drudgery. During the winter months, when mining slowed to a standstill, social activity warmed the hearths of those settlers who stayed within camp. The women visited while their hands were occupied with mending or quilt-making. The men gambled, whittled, and talked their way through the complexities of territorial politics. The Christmas-New Year season was especially precious to displaced Easterners who had learned at home the proper celebration of major festivals.

On special holidays, the entire town came together at the major hotels. At one hostelry they danced; at another they ate their fill of delicacies carefully hoarded and specially prepared. The usual solid staples (thick meat pasties, heavy sourdough bread, game-flavored venison and mountain sheep) were replaced on such occasions by fancy foods carefully set aside for just such celebrations. On these feast days, diners savored the unaccustomed luxury of thin-crusted fruit pies, soft, melt-in-your-mouth rolls, and thin slices of prime roast beef.

The people who successfully made the transition from East to West were invariably cultured, well educated, and fairly well-to-do. Simple survival demanded nothing less. The Christmas dance in 1862 at Buckskin Joe started with the overture from Bellini's "Norma," a score readily recognized by only the musically literate. The program that followed included jigs and waltzes, country tunes, and classical melodies.

While the townspeople reveled, relaxing from the rigors of their normal working habits, the Methodist minister, Reverend John Dyer, agonized, praying on his knees that the Lord would forgive the sinful dancing and the unrestrained gormandizing. On such occasions, these oh-so-human beings were of a different mind from their earnest evangelist. "If this be sinful," they countered, "then let us make the most of it!"

VI
Back to California Gulch

W hen the gold lodes at Buckskin Joe played out, the prospects at California Gulch shone brightly once again. As insatiable gold seekers and as practical sutlers, the Tabors followed the crowds to the paying mines. Over Mosquito Pass, in 1868, the Tabors moved their worldly goods. This time they took up residence in the camp called Oro City. During the next ten years, Horace was to operate three stores in the area: one at the upper gulch (Oro No. 2), one at the town of Malta, and one just below the lower gulch. This last location, generally known as Slabtown, eventually developed into the city of Leadville.

From Augusta's scrapbook we have a description and a comparison between the two houses the Tabors occupied while residents of California Gulch and Oro City. Augusta's newspaper clippings are undated and unlabeled, but they do supply valuable information. According to these items, the Tabors' original home was just a simple small cabin standing near the Oro Road. Although it had but one room, it was used for the family living quarters as well as for the mail room for the

entire town. The house the Tabors lived in after their return from
Buckskin Joe stood just to the left of Oro Road, a short distance from
where August R. Meyer later built his sampling works. This cabin was
far more pretentious than their first home. It, too, however, was made
of logs, roughly hewn. The building was a story and a half in height
and contained four rooms. Here the Tabors lived comfortably, with
adequate room for their well-stocked grocery store.

In Oro, Horace and Augusta repeated the habits learned during a
decade of living in Colorado mining camps. Through the years, Horace
had come to terms with his role as a merchant. Income from his stores
made him one of the wealthiest persons in the area. At this time, he
was probably worth between twenty and thirty thousand dollars. He
had time to continue his involvement with community and civic
affairs. As a sutler, he knew the location of every promising lode, and
he had the wherewithal to grubstake any miner with a handle into
pay dirt. Augusta was still sharing at least 50 percent of the workload,
clerking in the store, handling the mail, and providing board for
numerous customers.

In 1872, Horace picked up a contract to cut and supply railroad ties
for the Atchison, Topeka and the Santa Fe Railroad. This required the
labor of many men and the cost of shipping logs to Fort Dodge. It
proved an unprofitable venture, but at the time Horace's word was his
bond, and he insisted on fulfilling the terms of the contract. While
Horace was completely occupied with this work, Augusta was left to
handle all the business in Oro. The Tabors had the only safe in town.
Here Augusta stowed her profits along with any money that the townspeople entrusted to her for safekeeping. As Augusta admits, this was
not an easy time, and she struggled under the weight of such respon-
sibility for the five months that Horace was out of town.

In 1873, William Henry Jackson and his crew of photographers came
through Oro in the course of their work on the Hayden Survey. On
the expedition, Jackson had lost some of his glass plates. He headed
straight for Tabor's store, hoping that the proprietor might have picked
up a clue to their whereabouts.

The room into which Jackson stepped was a warehouse in miniature.
Three walls were lined from floor to ceiling with shelves crammed full

Oro City, lying in California Gulch, as it looked in 1873, a few years after the Tabors moved back from Buckskin Joe. The Iron Silver Mine would eventually be developed along the ridge at the right. *Colorado Historical Society.*

of merchandise. Horace, the sutler, boasted that he could supply every customer need from a pin to an elephant, and judging from the cluttered appearance of the store, it looked as though everything was available in open stock. There were mousetraps and marmalade, dry beans and lead bullets, sassafras tea and leather straps, curry combs and patent medicines.

Along the fourth side of the room ran a long, wooden counter burdened with whole hams, slabs of bacon, mounds of cheese, and open crocks of pickles, herring, dried apples, and prunes. In the center of the room, a squad of barrels, hogsheads, and piggins stood at attention, their bold black titles attesting to the incongruity of their place in line. Next to the kerosene stood the sugar; linseed oil was paired with blackstrap molasses. Toward the back of this room was a wired-off section clearly labeled POST OFFICE.

Horace emerged from his living quarters, hidden behind the wicket cage of the mail room. There was a meal bag tucked into his trouser top as an apron. As Jackson's son remembered his father's story years later, the conversation went something like this.

"Welcome, stranger. Tabor's the name. How can I help you?"

"I'm Jackson, William Jackson, of the Hayden Survey. I'm looking for some glass plates that I've misplaced. I'd hate to think they're gone forever."

"Glad to make your acquaintance, sir. I've been handling lots of government mail, thanks to your expedition. Always like the extra business. Sorry I can't help about the plates. If anyone here had come across them, I'd be sure to know."

As they were talking, a shabby, bewhiskered miner entered the store and shuffled his way toward Horace.

"Hi there, Hank," Tabor greeted the newcomer with a sigh of resignation. "Still need something?"

Lifting his boot, Hank said, "My foot is seeing daylight. It's tough trying to mine with so much water seeping into my socks. And — the grub's running low again."

"Got anything to pay with?" Tabor wanted to know.

"Don't look like it, Tabor, does it? But I'm getting closer. I swear. And when I make that killin', you'll be the first one paid."

Tabor turned to Jackson with a shrug. "I hear this day after day. If I had a dollar for every prospector I've grubstaked, I could vacation for a month in Denver."

Horace couldn't say "no" to a man in need, and there was always that slim chance that this one would find a bonanza.

"Okay, Hank. Take whatever you need." Turning his back on the self-serving customer, Horace focused his attention once more on Jackson.

Suddenly the rear door opened once again. This time a woman stepped into the store. She walked directly to Hank and Horace, confronting them. "Are you back again, Hank? And are you giving him another stake?" Her voice was crisp and cutting.

"Don't be too hasty, Augusta. Hank's got a sure strike. He'll be paying me back in a week."

"Is that so! Where's the strike this time, Hank? And no tall tales!"

"Just off Tennessee Pass, Mrs. Tabor. It won't be long now. I'm about ready to strike it."

Augusta groaned with exasperation. "Now both of you listen to me! You'll get your stuff all right, Hank, but we'll just keep track of it in writing."

Going over to the counter, Augusta took out a thick ledger and wrote down a few lines on an open page. "Now it's all listed and dated. All you have to do is sign, Hank. It's only a promise to pay and this way we'll have a record."

When the business was completed, Horace introduced Jackson to his wife. Augusta immediately extended a gracious invitation to supper. Unfortunately, Jackson was unable to adjust his schedule to accept her hospitality, even though Horace assured him he'd be missing the world's best cooking.

This story reaffirms the habit Augusta had of keeping accurate records for every money transaction. During all the years she handled the post office accounts, she was proud of the fact that only once had the United States Postmaster sent back a statement for correction. Her bookkeeping routine may well have helped define the difference between success and failure with the Tabor fortune.

By this time, Maxcy had begun to take his place as a trusted helper to his parents. By spring 1877, the son proved himself a capable partner in the family business, handling routine chores with efficiency and emergencies with mature aplomb.

According to Edward Blair in his history of Leadville, several dozen laborers from Detroit arrived in town in response to an advertisement for help placed by "Uncle Billy" Stevens. When Stevens and his business partner, Alvinus Wood, proved unable to fulfill the terms of the work agreement, the Detroit men angrily demanded at least fifty dollars apiece to defray their return fare to Michigan.

On the evening of May 11, 1877, the disillusioned workers decided

William H. "Uncle Billy" Stevens, who hid in the Tabors' store to avoid a lynch mob. *Colorado Historical Society.*

to force the issue with their would-be employers. Tipped off about the approaching hostile army, Wood and Stevens headed for the sanctuary of the Tabor store. Maxcy Tabor, then a young clerk of nineteen, was on his own that day taking care of his parents' business.

"For God's sake, hide us from that angry mob," the escapees pleaded. "They want hard cash, or our blood."

Maxcy helped Wood and Stevens hide behind the safe, while he calmly returned to his routine chores, rearranging stock on the open shelves.

Soon the cursing crowd, brandishing sticks, bats, and firearms, banged on the door, demanding to see the two men they knew were in hiding.

Maxcy stepped outside, shouting to be heard. "Now, boys, don't be so hasty. There's no call for violence. Don't you want to hear their side of the story?"

A bullet grazed the ground near the open door, spattering Maxcy with mud. "The only thing we want to hear is the sound of money in the till. We want our carfare home. Those lying bastards owe us plenty."

Pushing Maxcy aside, the brash, irate brood elbowed their way into the building, firing shots randomly into the ceiling and walls.

One rough character picked up a length of rope from the counter and started shaping it into a noose. "Come on, you dirty two-timers. We'll see how well you can dance at the end of this!"

Wood and Stevens sidled out from their ineffective retreat, flourishing coins and bills in their extended hands.

"You'll get what you want. Just give us time," they pleaded.

With Maxcy's help, the mob settled down. However, the men would accept no excuses. They wanted "up front money" and "now." Wood and Stevens sent a messenger to the Fairplay bank requesting funds from their account. Only when the dispatcher returned with the cash did the crowd disperse.

Fortunately, Wood and Stevens were not strung up by the would-be lynchers. These two professional miners were the first men to suspect, and then prove, that the lead carbonate prevalent in all the lodes from this area was a valuable product containing both lead and silver. It was this discovery that changed the miners' quest from gold to silver. It would be silver that made Leadville the mining capital of nineteenth-century Colorado.

During these years while Oro was becoming the nucleus for later Leadville, Horace was elected treasurer of Lake County. The Tabors were well off, well liked, and well respected. Later, Horace was to assert that this was one of the happiest stages of his life.

Both Horace and Augusta, individually and together, engendered many acts of kindness and generosity. They did this long before the "big strike" provided them with a superabundance of money. On more than one occasion, they opened their home to couples about to be married, providing them an attractive place in which to celebrate their nuptials. One of the families still living in Leadville will always be

Augusta Tabor, the successful merchant's wife, as she looked in the 1870s about the age of forty just before the great bonanza came in. *Denver Public Library, Western History Department.*

grateful to Augusta for providing the wedding facilities for Hezekiah Wright Rhodes when he took their grandmother Mary Dawson as his wife. Another wedding was celebrated for August R. Meyer, the successful metallurgist, who set up the sampling works near the Tabors' second home. Horace was best man for the ceremony and Augusta's sister Melvina was a witness.

In the early 1870s, Lottie Williams conducted an unofficial school in the original gulch. Miss Williams was a dear friend of Augusta, and years later she would board with Augusta in the Tabor mansion in Denver. During winter 1877, several months after the confrontation between the Detroit men and Wood and Stevens, Miss Williams, a Mrs. Updegraf (Leadville's first official teacher), a Mrs. Henderson, and Augusta Tabor formed a committee to provide a Christmas party for all the children in town. After the women had collected money to sponsor the affair, they discovered that toys and dolls were simply not available. Rather than abandon the project, the women bought every conceivable item that with liberal interpretation could be considered a gift. These Christmas goodies consisted of tin cups, tobacco plugs, shaving mugs, pipes, pocket knives, scissors, frying pans, buckskin mittens, clotheslines, and other useful notions. At least the children enjoyed the thrill of opening surprise packages. With plenty of popcorn, cookies, and punch available, the party was an unqualified success.

Horace had come into Colorado Territory in search of gold. He never lost faith in his dreams of sudden wealth. That dream was about to come true, served up to him on a silver platter. That annoying black sand which Augusta in the early years had tried so painstakingly to separate from the flakes of gold was, in fact, rich in silver-lead ore, which now interested all the miners. Leadville was about to be born, and, 10,000 feet high, it would be called Cloud City. For Horace A. W. Tabor, every cloud above his beloved city contained a silver lining.

VII
A Fabulous Fortune

The year 1878 was a pivotal one for Horace and Augusta Tabor. Horace at forty-seven years of age, and Augusta at forty-four, were settling into middle age. They were relatively content with their life and accomplishments. They were proud of their status in the community and their roles as pioneers of 1859. Horace had been elected mayor of this very important mining camp, which was soon to be christened Leadville. Augusta was an active participant in the social and civic events sponsored by the women of the community. She still ran a boardinghouse that brought in excellent returns.

In April 1878, Horace was dealt a winning hand. August Rische and George Hook, two prospectors who had persisted through unsuccessful digs in other camps, thought that they had a promising find on Fryer Hill, not far from the Tabors' store. But they were in need of more supplies to sink their exploratory shaft deeper into the ground. They first sought the help of the well-to-do Edwin Harrison, who was August R. Meyer's boss and president of the St. Louis Smelting and Refining Company — a business that was having a big impact on the boom. Unfortunately, Harrison was sick and unavailable the day that

Rische and Hook wanted the grubstake. The alternative was to seek
help from the ever-generous Horace Tabor.

One contemporary described Rische and Hook as "the worst played
out men I ever saw. Their total wealth consisted of a pick and shovel,
along with a yellow dog so wasted he had to lean against a rock to
bark." Nonetheless, they appeared no different from any other grubby,
hungry prospector, down on his luck, when they walked into the Tabor
store and asked Horace for a handout.

Horace was busy with a paying customer and simply directed them
to "take what you need." (He would later say that if he had known
where they intended to dig, he would possibly have refused them.)
Maxcy was clerking in the store that eventful day, and he helped the
two men assemble the needed tools, supplies, and grub. Legend says
that a jug of whiskey was part of the order (and that Rische and Hook
sat down under a tree, got drunk, and decided to sink a shaft there),
but Maxcy later denied it.

When Rische and Hook returned to Fryer Hill, they used Tabor's
supplies to sink their shaft deeper. Before long, they struck a vein of
ore fabulously rich in silver. Hook named it the Little Pittsburg after
his hometown, and by custom, Horace received a third of the take.
Riches poured forth. Tabor and a group of Denver bankers bought out
Rische and Hook, incorporated the Little Pittsburg Consolidated Mining Company, and paid sensational dividends. Mining experts said
that the Little Pittsburg produced $10,000 a day, and Maxcy later
recalled that the mine paid dividends of $100,000 a month for "quite
a long period." Horace eventually sold his shares for $1 million.

Once having tapped into this mother lode, Horace continued his
winning streak with other wealth-producing mines, particularly the
Chrysolite and the Matchless, both of which he acquired soon after
the Little Pittsburg bonanza. With this sudden, superabundant income,
Horace turned his attention to civic improvements, starting banks and
buildings, investing in public utility programs, and becoming involved
with local and state politics.

For Augusta he built a fine house on Harrison Avenue. He also
bought her jewelry and good furniture. For Horace the years of close-to-
the-vest living were over, but Augusta did not find it that easy to

The Little Pittsburg Mine, seen here at the height of its glory, formed the cornerstone of the great Tabor fortune. *Colorado Historical Society.*

The Chrysolite Mine, another jewel in the Tabor crown. *Colorado Historical Society.*

Harrison Avenue, main street of Leadville, in 1879. "Pap" Wyman's cabin still sat in the center of the street. *Colorado Historical Society.*

The Tabors' house on Harrison Avenue in Leadville, with a person, perhaps Augusta, watching the parade. A short time later, the house was moved to East Fifth Street to make way for the Tabor Opera House. *Luke and Wheeler Photo, Francis and Freda Rizzari Collection.*

change the budgetary habits of a lifetime.

In 1879, the Tabor house had to be moved up the road to East Fifth Street, where it still stands. On its site on Harrison Avenue, Horace was building an opera house that is also still standing in Leadville.

To compare the Leadville of 1877, when the carbonates were first mined, to the Leadville of 1879 is like sizing up polar extremes. In 1877, the permanent population was about 250. That figure increased steadily as silver mining met with continued success. By late 1879, the populace had exploded to twenty or thirty thousand people. There was not enough of anything — houses, hotels, streets, food, even time. People arrived in Leadville around the clock by any mode of transportation they could find.

Contemporary accounts paint Leadville as a city created out of chaos. Streets were so jammed with wagons and pedestrians that it sometimes took half an hour to push one's way from the north end of Harrison Avenue to the south end, which was only a matter of blocks. One gentleman wrote home to his wife, "I went down to Leadville yesterday to attend to some business and found it all sloppy and dirty and smokey. They are excavating through the main street for water pipes and dig down through the snow and ice. Then build fires up and down to thaw the ground so as to dig the earth."

Noted writer Mary Hallock Foote looked askance at the mushrooming camp, her Eastern eyes attuned to the amenities of civilization. She thought that going to Leadville was an "absurdity," and she was sure of it as she fought her way into the city. "The road over Mosquito Pass . . . began to look like the route of a demoralized army; there was no road — there were wheel-ploughed tracks upon tracks and sloughs of mud, dead horses and cattle by the hundreds scattered along wherever they dropped, and human wreckage in proportion."

Mary's friend, Helen Hunt Jackson, author of *Ramona*, had warned Mary to avoid Leadville. The place, she said, "was too unnatural. Grass would not grow there and cats could not live."

Augusta would have chided both women for lack of spirit. It was a waste of time, the experienced and adaptable Augusta would have told them, to concentrate on the mud at your feet when by merely lifting your chin, you could admire the cloud-strewn canopy of an outdoor

Chestnut Street in Leadville as it looked about 1879. Mount Massive looms in the background toward the west. *Western History Collection, University of Colorado Libraries.*

cathedral as it rested upon the flying buttresses of snow-encrusted mountains. It was all in the point of view. Leadville had its good points, too. It brought wealth and fame to many people and provided a broad economic base for the state of Colorado.

For the Tabors themselves, there was a lifetime of difference between 1859 and 1879. They had arrived in Denver as seekers after wealth. Now they were sought after. From the time of the Little Pittsburg discovery, everything Horace touched turned into money.

At this time, most of Augusta's family started to appear regularly in the Leadville directories. Rebecca's husband, P.J. Folsom, had been in the area since 1861. So had brother Frank and sister Lilly. Baby brother Fred came and joined the lumber firm of TABOR, PIERCE & Co. Sister Mary came with her husband Charles Marston, who had worked alternately as a lumberman with the Pierce brothers and as a grocer with Lilly's husband, Cyrus Taylor. Brother Edwin and his wife preferred to stay in Denver, where they later boarded with Augusta in her Broadway mansion. Sister Ruthe (Mrs. Peterson) made only infrequent visits to Colorado. Melvina, after she was widowed in 1871, spent much of her time with Augusta. In 1881, Horace sold the Leadville house to Melvina.

Augusta never forgot her early friends, even when she became one of the socially elite. One incident confirms this. The family from Augusta, Maine, most closely associated with the Tabors during the early years on the frontier was the Maxcy family. Nathaniel had come west with the Tabors, stayed with them in Kansas, and then shared their first adventures over the Republican Trail into Denver and up into the mining camps. In California Gulch, Nathaniel had become the mining district recorder and stayed on until the Tabors left for Buckskin Joe. By 1861, both his younger brother Ward and his sister Euphrasia had joined him.

An incident occurred in Park County in 1879-1880 that involved Euphrasia Maxcy and her husband John J. Hoover, as well as another person close to the Tabor story — Thomas Bowen, who eventually received the six-year term for United States Senator when Horace was assigned to the short term of thirty days. Hoover was one of the earliest arrivals at California Gulch. He moved with the Tabors to Buckskin Joe, but while Horace and Augusta remained at Buckskin until 1868, Hoover and his wife Euphrasia and brother-in-law Ward moved on a few miles further into the town of Fairplay. Here Hoover became proprietor of the Cabinet billiard parlor. As the *Fairplay Flume* reported, "He was of a violent and irascible temperament and when under the influence of stimulants (as was frequently the case) he was subject to no control. It has been held by his friends that he was insane, and this is the most charitable view that can be taken of the man."

On April 3, 1879, Hoover picked up a shotgun and without warning (and no provocation) murdered one Thomas Bennet, who was working on a ditch that had several times overflowed and washed down into Hoover's saloon. Bennet was simply a hired hand doing the bidding of the man who owned the ditch. The townspeople were outraged by the coldbloodedness of the killing. It was with the encourgement of his wife Euphrasia that Hoover gave himself up to the sheriff. Hoover was jailed for a year before he came to trial. Euphrasia now had no means of support and was also liable for her husband's debts. She opened a dry goods shop with the help of friends and family and tried to weather this misfortune.

Hoover was sure that he would be acquitted because he was a friend of Horace's. He boasted, "I'm a friend of H.A.W. Tabor and he'll see that I'm out in a year." That possibility was precisely what the people of Fairplay feared. When the trial finally opened with Thomas Bowen, Justice of the Peace, hearing the case, a vigilante group was formed. One dark night, they stormed the jail and dragged Hoover off into the night. When he pleaded for mercy, the masked men replied, "We'll give you the same chance you gave Bennet. None." The midnight avengers (as the local newspaper called them) took Hoover to the steps of the courthouse (which is still in use today) and dropped a rope down from a second-story window where the judge's chambers were. The knot was tied and Hoover was lifted up, kicking and strangling into the air. After an official inquest, the jury submitted this report: "We the jury find that John J. Hoover came to his death by being hung by the neck with a rope, suspended from the front window of the Court house in the town of Fairplay, about three o'clock in the morning of April 28, 1880. The said hanging was done by a party of masked men to the jury unknown."

At the same time that the masked men hanged the culprit, they left a coiled rope on the judge's desk. Judge Bowen either observed this omen early in the morning or was warned about it, because he never returned that term to Fairplay, and the event has gone down in Park County history as the "court that never adjourned." Famous as the case was, few realized the precise connection of the culprit with the Tabors.

Euphrasia Hoover, now a widow burdened with her husband's debts, was forced to sell her house and lot on Front Street. While her husband had been imprisoned, she had tried with indifferent success to support herself with a millinery shop. Now she had to depend on the generosity of friends. Evidently, Augusta extended financial support. She loaned money to Euphrasia. The amount of $856 was still owing at the time of Augusta's death. Obviously, this was another instance of careful

Lieutenant Governor Tabor, seated left, with Governor Frederick Pitkin, seated center, and other state officials in the late 1870s. This was about the time that the Little Pittsburg and Chrysolite discoveries made Tabor one of the richest mining men of his time. *Denver Public Library, Western History Department.*

bookkeeping. During the fifteen years that the debt was outstanding Augusta did not pressure her friend to make payment.

Augusta was ever mindful of the difficult years and the people who shared their common struggles. When Horace's miners struck for better pay and shorter hours, Horace took the part of management against the miners. Augusta supported the workers. She made her opinion known to her husband, but, like much of her criticism, he simply ignored it.

In 1878, Horace entered the larger political arena with his election as lieutenant governor of Colorado. His financial contributions to the

Republican Party's coffers gave him a certain sway. Also, he represented Leadville, which was now an important economic resource for the state. Because he would now have to spend considerable time in Denver attending to business at the Capitol, Horace bought the H.C. Brown mansion at Broadway and Seventeenth Street. On the evening of February 8, 1879, the Tabors made their official social debut by entertaining the legislature at an elaborate soiree at this elegant house.

The Tabors were in the receiving line with ex-Governor and Mrs. Routt. Large numbers of people invading her home was nothing new to Augusta. In pioneer days she had handled the mail crowds, weighed gold, and sold sow belly and beans in the one building that she had called "home." The new mode of living was in many ways a repetition of the old.

According to Flora Bishop, reporter for the *Rocky Mountain News* who covered the event, Augusta did not fawn over the important personages with whom she now mingled. About the February party, Miss Bishop later recalled, "One thing pleasant I remember on this occasion was the presence of several old ladies, not in any way courted by society, but who had been her friends in former years, and whom she did not choose to ignore for newer if more elegant ones."

In a later article for the *Kansas City Times*, this same reporter commented that Augusta was frequently criticized for allowing her servants to come into an adjoining room to listen and observe the festivities when she was entertaining the elite of Denver society.

Flora Bishop became Augusta's staunch friend. They were drawn together by a common interest in writing. Augusta expressed herself in her diary and sent occasional items back East to her hometown newspaper. Although she never became a journalist, Augusta's interest in the profession prompted her to attend the Colorado Press Association convention held in Manitou Springs in July 1879. Augusta kept a journal of the week's activities which Miss Bishop considered better than reports forwarded by other delegates to their respective papers.

The fact that the Tabors were now public figures left both of them open to community scrutiny and censure. Domestic unrest in the Tabor household became a common topic of conversation. One of the criticisms that surfaced was that Augusta could not adapt to the lavish life-style that Horace preferred. Augusta had come from a well-to-do family. What she obviously could not abide was careless and carefree overspending. Horace was not merely generous with his surplus money — he was prodigal. Still averse to maintaining careful records, Horace hired Lou Leonard to keep track of his accounts. After the decades of handling most of the money transactions, Augusta undoubtedly resented being shunted aside.

For years, Augusta had observed the miners in Leadville working hard all day in their digs, gathering a plentiful harvest from the earth, and then spending it all in one wild night of excess in the saloons and brothels of the town. "Easy come; easy go" was a pattern anyone could repeat, including the Silver King himself.

Now that Horace was no longer a common man, he yearned to forget the years of drudgery and dependence. Augusta was a constant, irritating reminder of where he had come from. With his head in the silvery clouds, the divine Horace resented any intimation that his feet were mired in mortality.

Augusta was as critical of Horace rich as she had been of Horace poor. Rebuffs that he had good-naturedly overlooked when he was young now became a major point of contention for Horace, proud and powerful. Marriage ethos of the nineteenth century decreed that a wife must accept and adapt to her spouse's deficiencies, but no reciprocal adjustment was ever expected of a husband for his wife's shortcomings.

Horace now resumed on a grand scale his earlier habits of drinking and gambling. He had a roving eye and a penchant for free and easy women. The entertainer Alice Morgan handled Horace as deftly as she swung her Indian clubs, although Erba Robeson, an actress at the Grand Central Theater in Leadville, claimed that Alice was frequently repulsed by Horace when he was drunk. He was particularly vulgar when under the influence of liquor.

A woman known as Willie DeVille followed Horace around the country after he had met her in a Chicago parlor house, and their escapades stirred clouds of scandal. At the time of his political campaign for lieutenant governor, even the newspapers insinuated that Horace had "two wives."

None of these dalliances was ever a prime issue with Augusta. To her, it was part of the "for better or worse" clause of the marriage contract. Nineteenth-century people operated on the double standard. A man was expected to sow his wild oats. His wife alone must carry the burden of docility, domesticity, and morality.

In 1879, the rift between Horace and Augusta widened. Although she was seen with him at various community functions, the couple spent more and more of their time apart. With most of her sisters and brothers now living in the immediate area, Augusta had friends to support and solace her. Horace was frenetically involved with his mining enterprises, his civic commitments, and his political aspirations.

Maxcy was actively participating in some of his father's programs. He became treasurer of the Leadville Grand Opera House and was appointed a member of the Board of Directors of the Bank of Leadville, which Horace founded and presided over.

The Tabors might have survived as a family by simply drifting along with and not fighting against the currents that were moving them in and out of the stream of social consciousness. They might have — except for Baby Doe.

VIII
La Femme Fatale

Elizabeth Bonduel McCourt (familiarly known as "Lizzie") was the fifth of twelve children born to Peter and Elizabeth McCourt of Oshkosh, Wisconsin. The family was fiercely Irish and devotedly Roman Catholic. All the children boasted fine features, attractive blue eyes, and blonde hair.

In 1883, the *Milwaukee Journal* had this to say about Lizzie: "[She] grew up in Oshkosh. She was a free and easy sort of girl, and hearty with the boys. She was considered as pretty loud, but all right."

In her twenty-third year, Lizzie was married to Harvey Doe against the violent protests of Harvey's mother. Lizzie's reputation in the small Wisconsin town was questionable, and Mrs. Doe wanted only a good girl for her son. More important, Mrs. Doe, a Protestant, was opposed to Harvey's mixed marriage in the Roman Catholic Church.

Harvey was decidedly a mama's boy. His chief attraction for Lizzie was evidently his ability to remove her from the wagging tongues of her home town. The very night they were married, Mr. and Mrs. Harvey Doe boarded a train that would take them to the gold camps of Colorado. Later, Lizzie admitted that when she left Oshkosh, she had "not one friend" except her father and her brother Peter.

In late June 1877, the Does arrived in Denver. After a short honeymoon in town, the bride and groom took the train to Central City, where they would live while working a nearby mine that belonged to Harvey's father, Colonel William Doe.

Flamboyant and irrepressible, Lizzie soon became well known in the mining camps of Central City and nearby Black Hawk. Here the miners dubbed her Baby Doe, not because she reflected the innocence of a child, but because she expressed the verve and vitality of a "babe."

In less than a year, Mother Doe's worst fears were realized. Lizzie took up openly with a storekeeper, Jake Sands (Sandelowsky). Jake was a handsome, dashing type of Romeo, and together they cut quite a figure. Jake squired Baby Doe to many dances, where the gossips reported on her behavior and her brashness. In her mementoes preserved at the Colorado Heritage Center, there are notes attesting to Baby Doe's love for Jake and the frequency of his kisses.

We cannot say for sure that Horace and Baby Doe met as early as 1878, but they certainly would have known about each other. Everyone in Colorado discussed the amazing luck of Horace Tabor; he was famous. In Central City and Black Hawk, everyone talked about Baby Doe; she was deliciously and daringly infamous. Horace's brother John, John's wife Hannah, and their son lived in Black Hawk during the 1870s, and as the *Central City Register* reported, Horace was a frequent visitor in their home.

According to William E. Roberts, a Denver firefighter, Horace and Baby Doe were seen together at various Firemen's balls during 1879 and 1880. An Oshkosh newspaper reported that Tabor met Baby Doe while she was still living with her husband; so these dates are probably accurate.

On July 13, 1879, Baby Doe gave birth to a stillborn boy. Rumor spread its lascivious lips whispering wicked insinuations about the child's paternity. Then, on March 2, 1880, in a surprising turnabout (considering the reputation Baby Doe had made for herself), Baby Doe sued for divorce. She charged Harvey with a single act of adultery committed in a house of ill repute in Denver. This brothel was located within walking distance of the Windsor Hotel, where Horace was now keeping Baby Doe in the lavish style she loved. Horace owned this hotel in partnership with William Bush, a close associate. Unfortunately, Augusta owned the hotel furniture, and it proved an embarrassment for Horace to have his wife on the premises at unscheduled times. He made a concentrated effort to buy out her stock and equipment. In the June 1880 census for Leadville, we also find Lizzie Doe living in a boardinghouse at 115 East Fifth Street, directly across from the Tabor residence. The Tabors were still using this home on their frequent visits to town.

In this same year, fourteen people were living at the Broadway mansion. Boarding others was still a way of life for Augusta. The only proper use for a twenty-room building, according to Augusta's practical lights, was to fill it with guests. Several of her family were boarding with her, along with the Erastus Hallock family and a couple of servants.

By January 1881, Horace had broken completely with Augusta and had moved into quarters in the Windsor Hotel. His most ambitious undertaking at this time was building the opera house in Denver. This project was the talk of the town. On September 5, 1881, the Tabor Grand Opera House opened to the delight and gratitude of the entire city of Denver. This was a fine way of bringing culture to the fledgling West. The building itself was a stunning architectural achievement for

Denver as it looked about 1880 when the Tabors took up permanent residency like most other successful miners. The Broadway mansion is at the far right. *Colorado Historical Society.*

Augusta Tabor in 1880,
shortly after she and Horace
moved to Denver.
Colorado Historical Society.

a city which little more than two decades earlier had been nothing
but a raw frontier town.

Two days before the anticipated opening night, Augusta painfully
penned this letter to her husband:

Denver, September 3, 1881

Dear Husband,

I am in town and would like very much to go to the Tabor Grand
and witness the Glory that you are to receive. Believe me that none
will be more proud of it than your *broken-hearted* wife.

Will you not take me there and by so doing stop the gossip that is
busy with *our* affairs.

God knows that I am truely sorry for our estrangement, and will

76

humble myself in the dust at your feet if you will only return. Whatever I said to you was done in the heat of passion and you know the awful condition that I was in when it was said. Pity, I beseech you and forgive me. And let us bury the past and commence anew. And my life shall be devoted to you forever.

Your loveing,
  Wife

Augusta recalled their years together and could find no vital reason why, if they had shared the travails together, they could not also enjoy the triumphs together. With this letter, she had done the difficult, humiliating thing. The next step was up to Horace. Evidently, he chose to ignore her pleas. On opening night, the Tabor box was empty. Baby Doe was somewhere in the audience. Horace stayed out of the limelight, occupying a seat in the parquet circle next to the last row until he was called up on stage to receive the appreciative applause of the first-night audience. Maxcy was present in another box along with his fiancee Luella Babcock.

As 1881 drew to a close, Horace became very impatient with the ties that bound him to Augusta, especially since the couple was no longer living together. Although he had separated from Augusta, that no longer was enough. Now he wanted to make Baby Doe his wife. Divorce was the obvious solution.

Horace was faced with a formidable challenge. How does one get rid of a wife who is unwilling to be divorced? For many reasons, Augusta was dead set against the dissolution of her marriage. No one in her large family had ever resorted to divorce, although several sisters had accepted separations of varying duration from their husbands. Rebecca Folsom had lived apart from her spouse for most of their married years. In considering the mores of the nineteenth century, divorce was a shameful stigma for a "good woman." For Augusta personally, divorce would be an open admission of defeat.

As the rift between them grew more irreconcilable, Augusta became fearful for her economic security. In March 1881, Horace signed a statement giving Augusta the right "to will her property to whomever she pleases." Two weeks later, Augusta wrote her will and had it witnessed. This was a step in the right direction, but as the wife of Mr. Tabor, she still did not have the autonomy of action she needed to ensure her future welfare.

Augusta realized the seriousness of her situation in 1882. Going to the La Plata County Courthouse in January, Horace, declaring himself a citizen of Durango, wrote a bill of complaint and asked for a divorce on those grounds. The decree was signed and is on file. No one has ever seen the original complaint, which was never served on Augusta, but in it Horace accused his wife of "every crime" except drunkenness. Adultery had to be one of the accusations, because the newspapers claimed that two prominent Colorado citizens were actually party to the crime. During the years when the double standard of behavior was prevalent, a wife's adultery was accepted unquestionably as sufficient cause for divorce. That is probably why the accusation was made. No one knows if Horace's charges *were* true. Certainly, in the years when Augusta was one of the very few women on the frontier, she would have had many opportunities to be unfaithful. No one has proved that she was.

Only once before the divorce do we find in print an implication concerning Augusta's fidelity. In February 1876, when some rival political faction was trying to discredit every prominent official of Lake County, an item appeared in the *Canon City Avalanche* accusing Horace of killing Augusta as she was eloping with Ward Maxcy, younger brother of Nathaniel Maxcy. A respected resident of Leadville, J. McPherson, refuted the report, saying that he had been at Granite with the Tabors on that day and that the entire story was untrue. McPherson ended his letter to the editor by extolling the virtues of both Horace and Augusta, declaring unequivocally that "the writer has yet to learn that she loves any one better than her husband."

The Durango decree was properly signed by an accommodating judge, but Augusta was not in the courtroom. She later swore under oath that she had never received a copy of the complaint. Horace's own lawyers advised him that the divorce could not be deemed legitimate because the circumstances were so suspect and so irregular.

The Durango intrigue alerted Augusta to the gravity of her situation.

William Bush, Horace's henchman, was coming almost daily to Augusta threatening that if she did not acquiesce to a divorce, Horace would cut her off without a cent, which was, of course, the husband's prerogative. With her liberal Maine training, Augusta knew that she was entitled to one-half of Horace's wealth. They had willingly shared the trials and tribulations of the lean years; the spoils should also be a fifty-fifty proposition.

Augusta appealed to the Colorado courts to sustain her in getting just and adequate financial support. She applied only for alimony and proper maintenance. In her complaint, she charged:

3. Plaintiff from the time of her marriage to the month of July 1880 lived and cohabited with defendant as his wife, and always conducted herself toward her said husband as a true, faithful and loving wife, forgiving her husband's faults and shortcomings, aiding and assisting him in their common business and sedulously striving to make their home and family pleasant, comfortable and happy.

4. That on or about the month of January 1881, said defendant disregarding the duty and solemnity of his marriage vow, wilfully deserted and absented himself from the said plaintiff and ever since has and continues wilfully and without cause to desert and abandon said plaintiff and to live separate and apart from her without sufficient cause or any lawful reason and against her will and consent.

5. That said defendant has oftentimes offered to the plaintiff a portion of his large fortune if she would apply for and secure a divorce between herself and her said husband from the bonds of matrimony, for which she has ample cause but each of said offers has been firmly rejected and is still declined by the plaintiff.

Augusta's bill of complaint also stated that by "their common, mutual exertions, patient industry and economy for more than twenty-three years, they had acquired property real, personal and mixed," all to the estimated value of $9 million. In this document, Augusta also said that Horace's present income was about $100,000 a month.

For herself, Augusta asked that the court declare the Broadway mansion her sole and separate property with the title vested in her name only. She also requested that Horace be ordered to pay $50,000 annually for her support and maintenance. But in the end, Augusta's suit was denied, because under Colorado statutes, there was no provision for alimony or for separate maintenance except in cases of divorce.

In answer to Augusta's claim that their property and wealth had been accumulated by their joint efforts and during her coverture, Horace vehemently protested "that he has accumulated all of this property since the year 1878 and mostly from mining, in the accumulation of which the plaintiff did not participate or render any material aid." With that statement, Horace glibly dismissed twenty-three years of married effort. This was a perfect example of the prevalent marital mores: "what's yours is ours; what's mine is mine." Horace's statement was not only callous, it was inaccurate. His bonanza in mining started with a grubstake from the sutler's store. Through the years, Augusta had been a full-time partner in that enterprise.

Although the suit for separate maintenance was settled in favor of Horace, that still did not get him any nearer to the divorce that he desperately wanted. For him, time was running out. In the latter half of 1882, he was busily engaged in running for the Senate seat vacated by Henry Teller, who had been appointed Secretary of the Interior. Within the Republican Party, Horace's rival for the senateship was Thomas Bowen, who had been justice of the peace during the trial of John J. Hoover.

Somehow, Horace convinced Augusta that their marital problems and the attendant gossip were hurting his chance for an appointment to the Senate. Augusta knew how very much Horace wanted this honor, and in spite of recent events, she was willing to do her part to help him. Against her better judgment, she agreed to sue for a divorce, charging desertion and non-support.

In later years, Augusta explained the series of events that propelled her toward the final separation. "They told me Mr. Tabor was very ambitious for the Senate, which I knew. He had been laying his plans for four years. I had helped him to lay them. I was told that unless I allowed a settlement and had it fixed up before the 9th of January, when they were going to ballot, Mr. Tabor would be defeated. If I would fix this maintenance up some way, he would go with all glory to the Senate and I was ambitious to help him. I thought perhaps it might be better for me to help him along."

On January 2, 1883, Augusta Tabor, alone (Horace did not appear in court), went late in the day to Denver District Court. Present in the room were Judge Harrington, County Clerk Steele, Sheriff Spangler, Horace's attorney Mr. Rockwell, and Augusta's counselor Amos Steck.

When asked by the judge if there was any collusion between herself and her husband in trying to procure the divorce, Augusta answered truthfully, "Yes." Mr. Steck hastened to interpret her answer. "Collusion exists only as to Mrs. Tabor consenting to take a certain sum of money to procure the divorce." That answer evidently satisfied the judge. He went on quickly to grant the divorce.

Then Augusta said, "Judge, I wish you would enter upon the record, '*Not willingly asked for.*' " Here her emotions surfaced and she burst into tears, protesting over and over, "Oh, God, not willingly, not willingly."

When Mrs. Tabor was handed a paper to sign, she turned to Mr. Steck and said, with an hysterical sob, "What is my name now?"

"Your name is Tabor, ma'am," he replied. "Keep the name; it is yours by right."

Knowing well the price she had paid for it, Augusta said, "I will. It was good enough for me to take. It is good enough for me to keep. I ought to thank you for what you have done, but I cannot. I am not thankful; but it was the only thing left for me to do."

If Augusta had wanted a divorce, or if she had wanted to hurt Horace, she would have sued for divorce on grounds of adultery, charges which could have been easily substantiated. Her own lawyer admitted, "She knows all about his practices with lewd women. If the truth were known, it would be enough to ruin Tabor forever. She knows all about it, yet loves the man so that she will not say a word. I never saw such a woman. She is crazy about Tabor. She loves him and that settles it."

Even Baby Doe's aunt acknowledged, "Mr. Tabor's first wife did not want a divorce on account of his unfaithfulness; it was he who procured one from her much against her will."

Augusta left the courtroom, still the possessor of the name Mrs. Horace Austin Warner Tabor. It was a pretentious name, but a hollow victory.

IX
On the Record

Soon after the Tabor divorce, Horace completed the race for the United States Senate. Thomas Bowen won the full six-year term; Horace was left to fill in the thirty days remaining from Henry Teller's unexpired term of office. Now his ulterior motive for the divorce was stunningly clear. He intended to marry Baby Doe in extravagant style in Washington, D.C., with President Chester A. Arthur in attendance.

Like the Biblical feast, many were invited; few came. Mrs. Nathaniel P. Hill, wife of Colorado's other senator, tore up her invitation and sent it back to the Willard Hotel where the ceremony was scheduled to take place on the evening of March 1, 1883. On the night of the wedding, President Arthur did grace the affair. According to the *Golden Transcript*, Senator-elect Bowen and members of the McCourt family were there. Maxcy Tabor also put in an appearance. He had accompanied his father to Washington and worked with him for the full thirty-day term. William Bush was there, but not his wife. The women especially were indignant about this vulgar trumpery and vented their scorn on Baby Doe. As to Baby Doe, all she wanted was the respectable title of senator's wife. It never crossed her mind that respect is not a free gift — it must be earned.

Horace Tabor, about the time
he married Elizabeth Bonduel
McCourt. *Colorado Historical
Society.*

Two days later, newspaper reports, like exploding bombs, shattered
the wedding bells. Every major paper across the country aired and
analyzed the scandal of a bogus marriage. It seems that the Reverend
Placide Chapelle, pastor of St. Matthew's Cathedral in Washington,
had been deceived and had unknowingly and against Church rules
solemnized marriage for a divorced woman.

Father Chapelle said that he had made a careful inquiry before
agreeing to the ceremony. Horace's divorce was not in question. He
was not a Catholic; so his previous marriage was not pertinent. Father
Chapelle had asked Horace the usual questions put to a non-Catholic
in a mixed marriage, but these involved his willingness to let Baby
Doe practice her Catholic religion and bring up any children in the
Catholic faith.

It was Baby Doe's first marriage that was at fault. Harvey was still alive, and therefore she was ineligible to be married in the Church. Baby Doe's father had submitted to the priest's inquiries. When asked if there were any impediment to the marriage, Mr. McCourt had said "No." As a practicing Catholic, he understood very well what the priest was searching for. It was a bold lie; it could not be considered like the lapse of memory he had when asked about the bride's age: "Twenty-two," McCourt had said. Baby Doe was actually nearly twenty-nine. But there were so many children in the McCourt family, such a miscalculation could easily happen.

The beleaguered priest returned the $200 gratuity for performing the ceremony and declared the marriage null and void. There has never been a record of the wedding in the files of St. Matthew's Church.

McCourt died less than two months after the Washington affair. His sister Ann was to write a letter blaming his death on the grief, guilt, and remorse he suffered over his part in this grievous deception. Evidently, Baby Doe had a tender conscience about it also. Although she felt especially close to her father, and although she was in Oshkosh for the occasion, she did not attend the funeral Mass.

After the exploding bomb, heavy artillery fire opened a final attack. A reporter dug up the fact that Horace and Baby Doe had been secretly married in St. Louis, Missouri, by a justice of the peace on September 30, 1882, six months before the Washington wedding. Why had they done so? Surely this would have been more damaging to Horace's senatorial aspirations than any gossip about his marital difficulties with Augusta. Why had these two undertaken so great a risk?

Baby Doe possessed $15,000 worth of jewelry and diamonds, most of them gifts from Horace. She had sent these items to her brother Jim in Oshkosh for safe keeping, and he put them in his safe deposit box in the bank. After a racing accident in September 1882, Jim was inconsiderate enough to die from his injuries. His creditors were knocking on the vault of the bank demanding payment for his debts. Baby Doe had to act quickly. Notwithstanding her grief at her brother's death and the possibility that she might wreck Horace's chances of becoming a senator, she had to regain those jewels and prove that they were hers — no easy task for a divorcee with no visible means

Elizabeth Bonduel McCourt "Baby Doe" Tabor, seen here in mourning for her father, about three months after she married Horace Tabor. *Colorado Historical Society.*

of support. Horace obliged. He married her and put up a bond that matched the value of the jewels. In a replevin suit, Baby Doe recovered her precious geegaws.

The point to be considered about the St. Louis marriage is that it was bigamous. Horace had been well advised by his lawyers that the Durango divorce was not legal. It was also bigamous for Baby Doe. Although her petition for a divorce was on file in Denver District Court, the actual decree of divorce was not entered into court files until 1886.

Meanwhile, on January 3, 1883, the day after Augusta's divorce, the Denver newspapers were filled with criticism of the district court's action. One reporter considered it "a great farce" and a travesty of justice. An unidentified lawyer opined, "That divorce can't stick. There is evident collusion there, and it should never have been granted." Another attorney promised to declaim against the granting of the divorce every time he could, because he believed a wrong had been done. Augusta's lawyer Amos Steck was widely criticized for his handling of the case. For weeks Augusta received widespread support.

Heartened by the public outcry, Augusta wrote the following letter to Horace:

January 31, 1883

Dear Husband:

I am happy to say that I am not divorced. And that you are still mine. All the intimidations and threats were of no avail, when I went into Court and swore that I had not consented to it willingly and I have since ascertained that the divorce is null and void. Now this is the 26th anniversary of our wedding. Just such a storm as we are having today, we were married in. And surely we did not live in a storm all those 24 years that you were at home!

Now you have the honors of the Senateship which you deserted me for. And when your month is out come home and let us live in harmony. Or I will come to you. There is no need of having our case

Amos Steck, whose handling of Augusta's divorce drew widespread criticism. *Colorado Historical Society.*

dragged through court again. And as I am your wife, I shall stand upon my rights.

I have consulted several prominent judges and they all tell me that it was a farce. Even Judge Steck will not tell me that it will stand.

Therefore, I subscribe myself your loveing wife

Mrs. H.A.W. Tabor

I really hope that you are satisfied and happy now.

Obviously, Augusta had no clue of the impending wedding of Horace and Baby Doe. It must have been a devastating blow when she realized how she had been manipulated and lied to. She had believed the go-betweens when they convinced her that her suit for separate mainte-nance was keeping Horace from the Senate. As to her determination to "stand upon my rights," that was futile bravado. During her lifetime, she seems to have salvaged only the right to be used and abused.

Augusta accepted the irrevocability of the situation. She took stock of her situation and made plans for the future. Now she was responsible for her own support. The only beneficial result from the divorce action was the return of her civil rights. As a single woman, she could now make contracts without asking anyone's consent. She could buy and sell property, and all the monies she earned were hers alone.

Although Augusta had originally wanted an assured income of $50,000 a year, the divorce granted her but two properties — the Broadway house and the La Veta apartments. These apartments, near Capitol Hill, were the most fashionable in town. They boasted massive marble fireplaces, ornate chandeliers, and formal parlors. There were fourteen apartments in the complex. Each rented for $100 to $150 a month. Augusta's income from these rentals would have been $1,400 to $2,000 per month. She also had income from boarders at the Broadway home. According to the paper that she signed on January 2, 1883, these two properties were worth $250,000 and were accepted "in lieu of all claim for alimony, maintenance, and support forever."

People have the mistaken idea that Augusta received a generous settlement. Tabor's income at the time was at least $1,000 a week, if not a day; he was probably the single wealthiest Colorado miner of his generation. After twenty-five years of servitude on the frontier, $250,000 can hardly be considered generous for so wealthy a husband. And the amount may have been even less. There is on file at the Denver District Court a signed deed which indicates that Augusta paid Horace $100,000 for all of Block 3 in the H.C. Brown addition, the property involved with the Broadway mansion. In 1880, Horace had given that amount of money to Augusta for her own use, and he may have wanted it back.

For a couple of months, Augusta contemplated going to court to have the divorce set aside. She hesitated because of the expense of the undertaking. Augusta frequently said, "Lawyers cost money." Likewise, the continued action was embarrassing for Maxcy, and this influenced her more than the outlay of capital. When asked by a reporter if Horace would live with her if the divorce were set aside, Augusta replied, "No, I couldn't hope for that; but it would be a great deal of satisfaction to me to know that that woman would be no more to him than she was before he gave her his name and mine."

From this perspective, after a century of time, it might give Augusta some slight satisfaction to know that the license for the Washington wedding was defective because it was never signed by a lawful minister. The marriage itself could possibly be considered illicit, depending on the disposition of any litigation to determine the legality of the action. That would mean that in spite of all the machinations, in spite of all the subterfuges, in spite of all the lying and double-dealing, Horace Tabor in his lifetime had only one legitimate wife: Augusta Pierce.

Basically, Augusta needed no reassurance from legal technicalities. Her philosophy is contained in a poem found in her scrapbook:

> The midnight sky and the holy gleam
> Of the stars are forever mated.
> The mingled waves of sea and stream
> Can never be separated.
>
> The words we speak as we loose our hands,
> With hearts that bend and quiver,
> Are just as futile as such commands
> Would be to the sea and the river.

Still forever the bond endures,
With resolute persistence;
And never a word of mine or yours
Can will it out of existence.

Though I loose my hand and say 'goodbye',
In vain is our weak decreeing;
There is no power that can break a tie
That is one with our very being.

Realist that she was, Augusta knew that no amount of lotus eating could obliterate the joy, sweat, and tears borne through the quarter century of a life shared and lived to the fullest.

The Washington license was indeed flawed, but it was probably the least defective element in a sordid scenario. A full courtroom of lawyers could have an exciting and extended field day discussing the legal ramifications and the pursuant implications of the Durango divorce, the St. Louis civil ceremony, and the Washington fiasco.

Only weeks after the Washington wedding, Horace had a falling out with William Bush, who had been his most trusted confidant and helper since 1878. Because of court cases involving both of them, much of the dirty Tabor laundry had been aired in public. The breakup of their friendship was due to two things. Horace was displeased with the way Bush had bungled the divorce, and he blamed Bush for all the inconvenience and humiliation that the divorce had cost him. Baby Doe encouraged him in dismissing Bush from his service. She wanted her brother Peter McCourt to be Horace's confidential secretary. More significantly, she wanted to punish Bush for his wife's refusal to acknowledge or accept her as a social equal.

In April 1883, just one month after the Washington wedding, Horace instituted a writ of attachment against Bush, claiming that Bush owed him about $20,000. Bush in turn claimed that Horace owed him money. It was in the course of these cases that details about the divorce were put on record.

Bush indicated that Horace had instructed him to gather information that could be used against Augusta in Horace's first suit for divorce in

Durango. On the witness stand, Bush admitted that he had lied about serving the summons to Augusta. He likewise asserted that Horace had promised him $10,000 for his help with the divorce. Such sum had not yet been paid.

In the course of the proceedings, Willard Teller (Henry Teller's brother), who was Bush's counsel, tried to establish Horace's character (or lack of it) by discussing some of the irregular proceedings involving the divorce from Augusta and the subsequent marriage with Baby Doe. As a result of this, the judge hearing the case reprimanded Teller for entering scandalous material in a case which should have dealt exclusively with nonpayment of debts. Teller protested that all he had discussed was the truth and what was public knowledge. When the judge complained that Teller was belittling Horace, Teller replied, "Belittle him? How? By stating facts which everyone knows to be true. There is nothing contained in that answer which is not true and if stating the truth was belittling the plaintiff, then I had a right to belittle him."

We have to assume that Teller wanted to get some of these facts in the record. In a contempt-of-court case, *The People* vs. *Teller*, he was fined $500 for his actions. However, Judge Dawson, in commenting on the scandalous material, gave a decisive and damning appraisal of some of the things that had happened to Augusta.

In his report, he wrote:

Among many other irrelevant, immaterial and scandalous statements therein, is the following:

"That the plaintiff (Tabor) paid to the said Augusta in such settlement the sum of about $400,000, and the said Augusta Tabor, though tearfully protesting on the witness stand, or at least in open Court, that she wanted no divorce, and had been forced into it by the plaintiff herein, yet so far consented that the Court granted a divorce to the said Mrs. Augusta Tabor; and the said defendant at once proceeded to repeat with the said Doe a marriage ceremony which had already, and before the said divorce was granted, been repeated between them, and has ever since and now does claim this last named woman as his lawful wife.

"If this language means anything it imputes to the plaintiff not only a gross violation of the civil law by coercing an unwilling wife to consent to a divorce, but also the crime of bigamy, by having procured to be repeated a marriage ceremony between himself and another woman while yet lawfully married. It goes further, and implies a grave charge against the Court which granted to that wife a divorce in the face of the fact that she 'tearfully protested on the witness stand, or at least in open Court, that she wanted no divorce, and had been forced into it by the plaintiff herein,' who was her husband."

There was some talk about impeaching Judge Harrington for his part in granting the divorce under the circumstances as described. However, nothing came of it, and Augusta's treatment at the hands of her husband and the court has rarely been criticized.

One of the penetrating statements made by Willard Teller at this time epitomizes the general consensus with regard to the second marriage of Horace with Baby Doe. Teller stated that the affair with Baby Doe was not so much a matter of bad morals as it was a case of "bad taste." That was exactly what society found objectionable about Baby Doe. She was not in "good taste." High society especially has a built in tolerance for infidelity. It is the gross and the vulgar that proper society finds insufferable. With the daily newspapers openly referring to Baby Doe as a "strumpet," there was no way that the proper matrons of Denver would accept her into their ranks.

X

Quiet Years

With the divorce, the real Augusta Tabor died. One of her relatives later said that after the divorce "Aunt Augusta was not the same woman." She went quietly about her business, helping those less fortunate than herself and playing a significant role in the Unitarian Church in Denver. In the difficulties with the divorce, Maxcy had sided with his mother, as did most of the old pioneers.

Maxcy's relations with his father were as amicable as could be expected under the circumstances until the Bush trials appeared in court. Choosing between his friend and his father was a more difficult option than standing by his mother. Maxcy and William Bush had been fast friends and business associates through the years from 1878 on. At the Bush trial, on the witness stand, Maxcy told the truth, and it contradicted his father's testimony. This caused the defense lawyer to say, "If Tabor is truthful, his son is a liar. If his son is truthful, Tabor is a liar." It was because of this action in court that Horace made the statement in a fit of frustration and anger, "Maxcy is no son of mine."

Maxcy lived with his mother at the Broadway mansion for several years. He was active in society of that day and owned a race horse,

Lady Bonner, that was a frequent winner on the Overland Park track. When he was getting ready to marry Luella Babcock, some reporter posed this question to Augusta. Knowing that she was very fond of her only child, the reporter wanted to know what Augusta would do if he, Maxcy, married a girl she didn't like. With no hesitation, Augusta replied, "Then I should try to like her because he did." That single statement, showing both a respect for her son's judgment and tolerance for a stranger, should qualify Augusta as patron saint of mothers-in-law.

Augusta made at least three trips to Europe, and her mode of travel was noted by the *New York Sun*, as found in her scrapbook. "A Colorado lady [who] is said to be worth a million but who was once a cook in a miner's cabin, is now traveling in Europe and has no agent or servants attending her. She attracts attention from her independent style."

In her final years, Augusta devoted most of her energies to the Unitarian Church in Denver and to her work with the Pioneer Ladies' Aid Society, of which she was a founder and officer. The latter organization was specifically designed to provide "assistance in poverty, comfort in despair, attention and aid in sickness, and fitting burial and death" to women who had come early into the territory and in spite of years of hard work were left bereft of family and fortune. As Augusta knew, the plight of destitute women was far more critical than that of men. She had seen much and learned painfully about the second-class citizenship of women.

When the Unitarian Church put up a new building at the corner of Tremont and Nineteenth streets, Augusta was one of the largest contributors to the project and the only woman among a group of wealthy men to subscribe. In one of Baby Doe's dreams (preserved in the Tabor collection at the Colorado Heritage Center), she reported dreaming that she and Horace were standing on the Brown Palace Hotel corner looking across the street at the proposed church site. Horace was so impressed by Augusta's generosity that he was feeling "very kindly" toward her. Baby Doe was fearful that Horace would divorce her and take up once again with Augusta.

Augusta was more of a realist. She knew that Horace would never willingly return to her, but she built up her fortune hoping that when he got into financial straits, as she was sure he would, she could lend

The Unitarian Church, which played so large a role in Augusta's later years. *Colorado Historical Society.*

assistance to him in his need.

It is to Augusta's credit that she never indulged in public diatribes against her husband. In fact, when she first started her scrapbooks, she rejected any items that were critical of him. She soon had to change her plan, because much of what was written about him in the

The Broadway mansion, Augusta's home in Denver for nearly fifteen years.
Colorado Historical Society.

late 1880s was abusive and scurrilous. One of the few statements she
ever made for the newspapers was said more in sadness than in spite,
"Mr. Tabor used to be a truthful man."

During these quiet years, Augusta directed her financial strategy
toward real estate. She picked up various parcels of land in metropolitan
Denver and the suburbs. She also purchased bonds from Senator
Stephen Dorsey, investing in his Chico Springs Ranch resort near
Springer, New Mexico. She owned 120 acres of land in Westminster,
Colorado — forty acres where the university buildings were situated
and the contiguous eighty acres to the north which comprised the
college farms. She also owned land at Sixteenth and Lawrence streets
in Denver, where the Golden Eagle Department Store was located.

In 1890, she amended her will, not revoking any significant portion
of it, merely making some minor additions and changes.

In 1893, she leased her Broadway mansion to the Commercial Club
of Denver and moved across the street to the Brown Palace Hotel,
which Maxcy was then managing and where he lived with his wife
Luella. Their daughter Persis Augusta was born there the following year.

96

In the 1890s, Augusta shared much of her time with her sisters and brothers and their families. She was especially fond of her nieces, Susie Marston and Vesta Folsom.

As a pioneer, Augusta made a significant contribution to Colorado and its history of the West. It would be difficult to match the excitement, energy, and enterprise of the early years. By comparison, the later years of her life seem lusterless. She did not, however, slip unobtrusively into that "last good night" without making a valuable contribution to the city of Denver.

The Unitarian Church in Denver had its beginning when a Reverend Mr. Beckwith held a service one Sunday in 1871. Finding here the

Denver in the mid-1890s, about the time of Augusta's death. The Broadway mansion lies hidden in the trees at the right across the street from the Brown Palace Hotel. Compare this with the photograph on page 75 to see how Denver had grown in fifteen years. *Colorado Historical Society.*

Nathaniel Maxcy Tabor,
about the time he managed
the Brown Palace Hotel.
Laforgue Private Collection.

nucleus for a congregation, he asked city officials to permit him tc
hold services in the courtroom, then located on Market and Sixteenth
streets. During these early years, the congregation also held services
in the Methodist Seminary at Fourteenth and Lawrence streets, in the
Baptist "Dug-out," in the Denver Theater at Sixteenth and Lawrence
streets, and for a couple of Sundays in the Colorado Seminary. As
one member reported, in the first two and a half years of its existence,
the Unitarian Church had met in seven different places ranging from
"bad to unspeakable." In 1873, tired of wandering, the congregation
decided to build its own church, not to cost more than $10,000.

Activating the church and inspiring the congregation were persistent
challenges against the allure of lethargy and the powers of darkness.
Within ten years of its inception, the men who controlled the church
board abandoned their leadership, saying that the church could not
possibly survive. They turned the church building, its large liens, and
its few assets over to the women with this advice: "Sell the property,
pay the debts, and consider the effort to establish a liberal church in

Members of Augusta's family on holiday. *Amon Carter Museum, Fort Worth, Texas.*

Denver a failure." The women were unable to swallow the word "quit." They had survived the frontier; they knew they could sustain the church. They raised funds slowly and simply through a succession of strawberry festivals, dances, teas, and sales of home-crafted goods. There were no high finances, just a deep belief in their church and in themselves. In a matter of years, they had saved the church and were planning to put up a new building at Broadway and Nineteenth, which would be designed by Frank Edbrooke, a noted architect.

The Ladies' Aid Society of the church did a tremendous amount of charitable work. In the early days, it carried the burden of church support after the men surrendered the responsibilities to them. It was this society which sustained the church and kept it alive. The women gave continuous assistance to the Women's Hospital, the Foundlings' Home, and the Free Kindergarten. They not only gave clothing to the poor of the city, but they brought in the girls of poor families and taught them how to sew, knowing that the teaching of a skill was a better and more lasting contribution than the mere gift of attire. They

Augusta Tabor about the age of sixty. *Denver Public Library, Western History Department.*

held night classes in reading and writing for the newsboys of the city, who were busy during the day earning their pennies for the family's support.

Augusta's name is contained on many pages of the files and records of the Unitarian Church. She was active on all kinds of committees. She freely offered her Broadway mansion for teas and festivals, and these always proved very popular and were effective money raisers. One such gala occasion was described at length in the minutes of the Ladies' Society records, and it gives a pleasant picture of the Tabor residence:

The 3d annual Lawn Festival of the Unity Ladies' Aid Society took place on Thursday evening June 17th (1886) on the beautiful grounds at the residence of Mrs. Augusta Tabor, Lincoln Avenue. The lawn, always sufficiently attractive, was rendered doubly so by being brilliantly illuminated by 72 chinese lanterns and four locomotive headlights.

The full moon also lent the silvery light of her countenance to the scene which was almost fairylike in appearance. The evening proved most auspicious for the occasion and some 300 people assembled to enjoy the lovely festival.

Dainty tables were set on the lawn; for each table, a bouquet of choice roses and other flowers prepared by Mrs. Tabor. The young ladies of the congregation in pretty costumes flitting hither and thither heightened the beauty of the scene while courteously serving every guest.

The doors of Mrs. Tabor's beautiful home were thrown hospitably open and a fine program of vocal and instrumental music added to the attraction of the evening.

The secretary feels that she but voices the thought of all the Ladies of the Society when she expresses in the highest terms their appreciation of Mrs. Tabor's kindness and generosity in thus opening her house and grounds to the Unity Church and their friends for these lovely lawn festivals.

Mention of the floral decorations prepared by Augusta points up her lifelong interest in gardening. In Buckskin Joe, Samuel Leach admired her skills. Even in the Broadway mansion, she attended to her own yardwork, although gardeners were also employed. For many years she exhibited her produce at the annual agricultural fair held in Denver. Once she brought stalks of sweet corn that stood fourteen feet high. Her Concord grapes consistently earned top awards. Augusta, still the animal lover, even exhibited a huge mastiff dog whom she christened Henry Ward Beecher. The name was a reminder of the days in Zeandale when Horace and his cohorts carried guns in the war against slavery, as Beecher had encouraged.

A train excursion was another fund-raising event in which Augusta was involved. On June 18, 1893, she organized a trip to Colorado Springs and Manitou Springs, including side trips to the Garden of the Gods and Glen Eyrie. One hundred and sixty-one tickets were sold, netting several hundred dollars of profit to the church. One pastor admitted that this particular group was the most earnest, the most devoted and the most self-sacrificing band of women he had ever known. Without their resolution and their persistent endeavors, the Unitarian Church might not have survived.

The church members not only appreciated Augusta's financial help, they loved her as a friend. It was this particular group that organized a surprise party for Augusta in April 1883 to help her through the trauma of the widely publicized Washington marriage of Horace and Baby Doe. It was with their encouragement, support, and friendship and the spiritual guidance of the church's pastor, the Reverend A.M. Weeks, that Augusta was able to endure the difficult years surrounding the divorce and the defection of her husband.

Reverend Weeks was a popular minister of the church, but his tenure lasted less than two years — from 1882 to 1884. He supported Augusta in her belief that marriage was forever and bolstered her resolve never to be married again. On January 29, 1884, Weeks (who was one of a dozen boarders at the Broadway mansion), died suddenly in his thirty-third year at Augusta's residence. He had been engaged to a Miss Gerrick and had planned to return to his native New Hampshire during that year and marry her.

Although Augusta was most active with this group and with the

Pioneer Ladies' Aid Society, she was frequently reported in the newspapers as attending socials sponsored by the leading matrons of the day. Her dress was invariably described as subdued rather than somber, and her jewelry was inconspicuous and in good taste.

The Unitarian Church building to which Augusta so generously subscribed was later torn down to make way for a rent-a-car establishment. Buildings have a way of disappearing from the local scene. Leaving a building for posterity has a dubious future merit. However, an institution such as the Church itself is of lasting effect and value to succeeding generations.

Augusta's disposition was ecumenical. In 1884, she loaned Father Machebeuf, director of the Catholic Church in Denver, the sum of $1,250. According to local history, Augusta had nursed Father Machebeuf through a siege of mountain sickness in the 1860s. This may have been the reason he sought her help when he needed money. He also respected her ability as a businesswoman.

Augusta was true to her marriage vows. Only death delivered her from the bonds she accepted on January 31, 1857. In a way, the name she bought so dearly and fought so hard to keep remains peculiarly hers. Legend has burdened her successor with the title "Baby Doe." Perhaps an avenging angel condemned Lizzie McCourt to be bound forever to the propriety of her only legitimate marriage.

In the year 1894, the Pierce family suffered multiple losses. Two of the Pierce brothers died, just months apart. These were the first family losses since Vesta had passed away forty years earlier. Fred died in Leadville in September 1894. His body was shipped back to Augusta, Maine, where he and his wife rest in the large family plot.

Edwin died in Denver on Christmas Day 1894. He had remained near the Maine homestead until 1867, when he and his wife moved to Concord, New Hampshire. Here they resided for the next twelve years. In 1879, Edwin came to Denver, primarily for reasons of health. He went to work for Horace (then lieutenant governor) at the Capitol in some clerical capacity. Later, Edwin took over management of the Clifton House, a hotel located on the corner of Arapahoe and Seventeenth streets. Frank Edbrooke designed a charming house for Edwin and Frances Pierce at 2147 Grant Street, where they were living at the time of Edwin's death.

By 1894, Augusta was suffering from a persistent cough, and her respiration was labored. According to one newspaper, she was also afflicted with a numbness akin to paralysis. This must have been particularly irksome to the active Augusta. In search of milder weather, she went to Pasadena, California, for the winter months. She took up residence in the Balmoral Hotel at the corner of Fair Oaks and Dayton streets. This hotel (originally known as the Acme) had been constructed in 1887 and was widely acclaimed for its architectural use of stucco over brick to give the effect of cut stone. It was a first-rate hotel but not ostentatious, like the neighboring Hotel Green. The Balmoral provided the type of quiet quality Augusta would have been comfortable with.

The cough did not respond to the mild climate, however, and Augusta's condition worsened. During the last week of January 1895, she came under the care of a Dr. Macomber, but he could neither reverse the course of her illness nor improve her physical debilities. Augusta, alone, far from family and friends, slipped unobtrusively into the last frontier. She died on January 30, 1895, the eve of her thirty-eighth wedding anniversary. She was in her sixty-second year, but Macomber, who had known her only a few days, wrote on the death certificate, "60 years of age."

According to Macomber, Augusta's death was caused primarily by chronic bronchitis and secondarily by pneumonia. Historians have used February 1, 1895 as the time of her death, undoubtedly picking up the dateline when the item arrived at newspaper desks.

Maxcy went to Pasadena and returned to Denver with the body of his mother. Lizzie McClelland, a member of the Pioneer Ladies' Society, had been living at the hotel, and she helped Maxcy with some of the final details.

In her basic wardrobe, Augusta had no dress suitable for burial, so the undertaker in Pasadena swathed the body in folds of soft white material. When the body arrived in Denver, Maxcy's wife said that she didn't like the effect. They obtained an orchid blouse from Augusta's sister-in-law Frances Pierce, and in that borrowed finery Augusta was buried.

On February 8, 1895, the funeral was held in Denver. During the morning hours, the body reposed at the home of Frances Pierce at 2147 Grant Street. From there the remains were taken to the Unitarian Church at Nineteenth and Broadway, the same building that Augusta had supported so generously. The church was crowded beyond capacity. There was a special section set aside for members of the Pioneer Ladies' Aid Society. Many of the pioneers themselves were in attendance, including Mrs. Charles Hall, one of the first women to join Augusta in South Park during the gold-rush days. Horace could not have been there or the newspapers would have commented upon his presence.

The Reverend N.A. Haskell gave the eulogy, which stressed Augusta's role as a pioneer: "Born of that sturdy New England stock, imbued with a hardy spirit that endures without complaining, she left the borders of civilization to go out away from home and friends, out into the wilderness, here to open the way to a new civilization. Perhaps there is not even a man in this state who has done so much to open the way into the wilderness as she who lies here. Her name will ever be associated with the history of this state and of this beautiful city." Haskell also used the term "respect" in describing the feeling that most people had for Augusta, and well she had earned that appraisal. Even people living a century later in Zeandale, Kansas, said that their grandparents spoke of Augusta "with respect."

Then Augusta was buried at Riverside Cemetery. Eventually, stonemasons erected a marker that reads:

AUGUSTA L. TABOR

1835-1895

Of course, she had been born in 1833. The reason for the error probably lies in her doctor's guess that she was sixty years old at the time of her death; the stonemasons simply subtracted sixty from 1895.

Augusta would not rest alone. Her sister Lilly joined her at Riverside in 1925.

Augusta's estate was divided between her son Maxcy and her sisters and brothers. Headlines in the Denver papers claimed that she left an estate of one and one-half million dollars — a figure very close to the mark.

Augusta had sold the La Veta apartments in the 1890s for $207,000. The Broadway mansion was sold after her death for close to $150,000. The Westminster property was valued at $106,000. These three properties alone were worth close to half a million dollars. Various small pieces of land in Arapahoe and Jefferson counties were valued at $100,000. Two valuable pieces of real estate would not be settled until after the deaths of the occupants. These two properties (one an apartment house and the grounds fronting on Lincoln Street, the other a residence on Vine Street) would eventually go to her nieces. She owned several mines in Lake and Park counties. She held an interest in her father's old homestead in Maine, and she owned an apartment house with two rentals in Portland, Maine. Her sister Rebecca had lived in this house for many years. Augusta's cash stocks amounted to $21,000; jewelry, $4,000; household items, $1,200. Leopold Guldman was paying Augusta $700 a month rental for property on which stood his Golden Eagle Department Store. From the Augusta Tabor estate, Guldman eventually purchased the lots for $80,000. She must also have been receiving rent from the Commercial Club, which was leasing the Broadway mansion at the time of her death. The largest figure in her estate was for $315,000, which represented monies owed to her. This amount undoubtedly reflected the caliber of her generosity. Most of the money was on loan to family and friends, and Augusta never really expected full payment.

From what Augusta received in settlement for the divorce, she had painstakingly increased her fortune until she was one of the wealthiest women in Denver. Augusta successfully weathered the financial panic of 1893, which ruined many financiers, including Horace. From the late 1880s, his fortunes had been on the decline due to extravagant living, overextension of credit, and some risky mining ventures. The Panic of 1893 was the final blow for him.

Augusta had accumulated all of her wealth from sweat and labor, and the careful husbanding of her resources from the beginning years of her life on the frontier. The Zeandale property, which held a sentimental value for Augusta, was never legally hers. Horace's brother

Lemuel sold it just before the turn of the century, but the house that Horace built for his growing family still stands.

Augusta died peacefully, knowing that she had never compromised her integrity. Both Horace and Baby Doe died tragic deaths, like protagonists in a Greek tragedy. At the purported marriage in Washington, D.C., Father Chapelle had said, "No good can ever come from such black deceit." His words were prophetic, foretelling the doom of an inexorable fate. On April 10, 1899, when Horace died of appendicitis, there was not enough money in his estate to pay the funeral expenses. Baby Doe lived on until March 1935, when her frozen body was found in the wooden shack that had stood for years above the once-rich Matchless Mine. She, too, was a pauper.

*　　*　　*

As a resident or a tourist, take a drive into the Colorado mountains. The highways are smooth and safe; the scenery in winter or summer is spectacular. Try to envision such a trip in 1859! No roads, no maps, no wayside inns, no air-conditioned cars, no comfortable motorhomes. The imagination would be stretched beyond credulity. How did the pioneers do it?

They were a hardy, determined people, these pioneers. We should never underestimate their heroism, nor fail to appreciate their enduring gifts. What they accomplished is our proud inheritance.

The men came, driven by a desire for wealth, an ardent wish for adventure, a firm belief in finding what was "better." Their women came because they had to. No matter how timid, how fearful, how emotionally unsuited, how physically frail, the women came because they were helpmates, and it was their duty. What the men did was considered exceptional; what the women did was expected of them.

Horace and Augusta Tabor traveling to the uncharted West with their child are a symbol of all plucky, persevering pioneers. We admire them the more when we recall that "the cowards never started and the weak died on the way." They forged their own roads; they built homesteads; they helped the less fortunate; they founded cities; they set up governments; they established schools; they subsidized churches.

They were the foundation, the building blocks, of a civilization. And it is here that we find the genuine romance in the Tabor saga: a young husband and wife sharing their love and their strengths to adventure into the wilds and subdue the wilderness.

Augusta Tabor is special because she left us an arresting and accurate account of a woman's life on the frontier. She illustrated the strengths and stratagems needed to survive the hostile land and improve it. Her story is the story of countless women who did the same. For every woman who left a comfortable home for a wretched lean-to, for every woman who exchanged society for solitude, for every woman who surrendered the security of the known for the uncertainties of the unknown, for every woman who steadfastly supported her spouse through the lean years only to be abandoned by him in days of plenty, Augusta speaks.

There are those who say that Augusta did not love Horace enough and that is what drove him into the arms of another. Horace would be the first to admit that he much preferred wide blissful byways to a confining path of the straight and narrow. Augusta would protest, echoing the words of Golde in *Fiddler on the Roof* — "For twenty-five years I lived with him, fought with him, starved with him; for twenty-five years my bed is his. If that's not love, what is?"

Augusta put duty first. She loved Horace by giving him stability, purpose, devotion, revenue. Training had taught her to do what she should do, rather than what she would do. The Tabors' tragic flaw was that Augusta provided what was necessary, and what Horace needed was not what he wanted.

Contemporary Comments

"There is no doubt that much of Tabor's success was due to her courage and strength of purpose."

— *Chicago Tribune*, January 23, 1898

"He [Tabor] and his wife did all the work about the little store and hotel [in Oro] and it was a general rendezvous for all the men in the gulch, and the mountains about. The Tabors were always willing to give a man a night's lodging and groceries, whether he had money or whether he had it charged. No one will ever know how many indigent people they helped out."

— William N. Byers, editor *Rocky Mountain News*

"Mrs. Tabor is one of the pioneers of Colorado and is just the same now while enjoying great wealth as when it was but in anticipation. Her beautiful Denver home is always open to miners and 'plain people' she has known. Her one son, by force of a judicious training, is now one of the best young business men in the country."

— Item from the *Silver Cliff Miner*

Mr. and Mrs. Sam Gill (he was an officer in the Bank of Gunnison owned by Tabor) named one of their children, born April 30, 1881, Augusta Tabor Gill. This is a token of the highest esteem and love to name a child after an acquaintance when so many relatives hope for that honor.

"My father Frank Myers was personally acquainted with Horace Tabor, the first Mrs. Tabor and Baby Doe. I've heard him tell what a sweet, respectable woman Augusta was and how she stood by Tabor when he was nothing."

— Mrs. E.L. Ely, Fort Morgan, Colorado

"Augusta was an angel of mercy whose infinite kindness of heart and acts of benevolence were legion."

— Nathan Hurd, pioneer

Writing about Tabor's rise to wealth: "This was the beginning of his fortune, and his wife did her part toward winning it by economy, self-sacrifice and hard labor. She was an excellent woman. She was a typical frontier woman, keeping 'hotel', cooking and washing. She was as industrious as her husband, and as generous. Many a night they gave a needy miner lodging, and they furnished groceries to fellows in hard luck, never expecting anything in return."

— Eugene Parsons, *Trail Magazine*

"She is admired by strangers as well as friends. She is known as 'The First Lady of Leadville.' "

— *Leadville Chronicle*, August 31, 1879

"Few women were more thrifty or industrious. Not many men had more courage, common sense, or initiative, especially in a crisis. While not a large woman, she had great strength and remarkable endurance. Augusta was more than a helpmate to Tabor. She was a full fledged partner, and often carried more than her share of the mutual load. Moreover, without her restraining influence in his younger days, it is quite likely that Tabor would have degenerated into one of those aimless, worthless men always found in large numbers in any mining camp."

— *Morning Chronicle*, Manhattan, Kansas

"Mrs. Tabor was tall and not ungraceful in appearance. Her features were somewhat angular and she lived such a quiet life that many citizens of Denver did not know that the lady in black who passed along without the slightest ostentation or display was one of the wealthiest women in the West. It is said that Mrs. Tabor was the principal in many acts of charity, but she seldom talked upon the subject to her friends and the world will never know the extent to which she distributed her wealth for the alleviation of distress. As a pioneer woman she performed her part in paving the way for the advantages which are presented today. No other woman of Colorado has developed the financial ability which marked the course of Mrs. Tabor for ten or fifteen years. With her departure passes from the stage an historical character of the state."

— Death notice in Denver papers

"She [Augusta] was a sterling character."

— *St. Louis Globe Democrat*, 1895.

February 10, 1895. Resolution of Pioneer Ladies Aid Society:

Resolved: That in the death of Mrs. Augusta Tabor we realize that we have lost an efficient co-worker and sympathizer in all the purposes for which we are banded together; a charter member, one of the first board of officers, thrice re-elected to a position among the honored officers of the society; she was always ready to perform her share of the necessary work in caring for her fellow pioneers in need of assistance.

Resolved: That we bear full testimony of our appreciation of the womanly qualities evidenced by her life in the various vicissitudes of an eventful career, through poverty and affluence, in the furnace of affliction, bearing the burden of life with courage and fortitude with meek and quiet spirit, gentle, unassuming, forgiving, charitable.

Contemporary Comments:

William N. Byers: quote fround in FF 1350, Tabor File, Colorado Historical Society Library.

Silver Cliff Miner: Augusta Tabor Scrapbook, Denver Public Library, Western History Department.

Sam Gill: *Gunnison Review Press*, April 30, 1881.

Mrs. E.L. Ely: Mundhenk Scrapbook, Denver Public Library, Western History Department.

Nathan Hurd: Interview, December 11, 1921, Colorado Historical Society Library.

Eugene Parsons: *Trail Magazine*, Vol. XIV, No. 5, p. 7.

Morning Chronicle: Undated excerpt, Riley County (Kansas) Scrapbook, p. 36.

Background
Material

$\mathbf{T}$he major portions of this book are based on materials in the Augusta Tabor scrapbooks that I found in France, and on three versions of her reminiscences. One of these is contained in Alice Polk Hill's *Tales of the Colorado Pioneers*. The second is titled "Cabin Life in Colorado" and was published in the *Colorado Magazine*. This latter account is based on an original interview with historian H.H. Bancroft in 1884. The third version remains with Philippe Laforgue and came to him through his mother Persis Tabor, daughter of Maxcy and Luella Tabor. All three overlap, repeating some of the same information. The third version contains some information not found in the first two.

Reminiscenses of Mrs. Augusta Tabor

My first acquaintance with H.A.W. Tabor came about in this way: My father, a stone contractor, wanting more stone cutters, took the train one morning for Boston. At a station forty miles from home two young men got on the coach that my father was on and took a seat beside him. In conversation he remarked that he was going to Boston to hire stone cutters. They were both going to Boston to get a job. Father hired them then, and they left the train at Portland and came home at Augusta.

That was in the year 1853. Two years from that time, he, H.A.W. Tabor, asked me to marry him. Two years more we were married. In the meantime he had gone to Kansas and squatted upon 160 acres of farming land. Immediately after we were married we came west from St. Louis to Kansas City on a boat. There we purchased one yoke of oxen, bought a little provisions, a few farming implements, some seed, and then drove into Kansas about 100 miles westward.

We arrived at our destination on the 19th day of April, having been out from my home since the 25th day of February. We were nearly three weeks going from Kansas City to Zeandale. The cattle were thin and the grass was poor.

I shall never forget the morning of my arrival. To add to the desolation of the place, one of the [Kansas] winds was blowing furiously. Sitting upon an open prairie, one-half mile from any cabin, was my future home — a log cabin 12 x 16 feet, not an outhouse, or a stone, or a stick in sight. I was ushered in, and the only piece of furniture in the room was a No. 7 cook stove that was confiscated from the border ruffians' brotherhood. I sat down upon an old trunk, the only thing to sit on, and the tears began to flow copiously. Why I felt so badly I could not tell for I had not been deceived. I knew just the size of the house. I also knew that it stood out upon an open prairie. I could not realize how lonely it could be. Then we had seen so many Indians on our way, and I feared them.

Mr. T. busied himself with unloading the wagon, then made three three-legged stools, a table, put up a shelf for dishes. I felt badly to think that I cried, for I knew just what I was coming to. After a few hours I dried my tears, cleaning up the cabin and prepared the first meal that I ever tried to cook. There came with us from Augusta, Maine two gentlemen, so I took them to board and commenced house-keeping with two boarders. The men were kind to me and assisted me with the cooking, which consisted most of the time of "Hog and Hominy" with corn bread and milk for a change.

We put in seed and tried farming, but there was no rain, so when fall came with harvest time there was not much to garner. Mr. T. went to Fort Riley and worked at his trade, while I stopped at home and kept watch and ward. In the month of October, baby came to live with us.

The spring of 1858 we tried farming again. Had an abundant crop in the fall, but no market. Eggs were three cents for a dozen; corn, shelled 20 cents at the Fort which was 20 miles away, so it took two days to haul a load and return — a slow way of making money. I kept my two boarders and made butter from one cow to sell.

The snakes were a terror to me in Kansas. They would come into my house, get onto my bed, secrete themselves on my milk shelves. In fact, all Kansas was alive with them.

In February 1859, Mr. T. first heard of Pike's Peak through some one of Green Russell's party who was returning. He concluded to try his luck. He told me that I might go home, but I refused to go, and upon second thought he concluded that it would be best to take me, for if he took me to cook, he could get those two men that had been with us all the time to go and board with us, and their money would keep all four of us. Mr. T. worked at the Fort through March and April to get the money to outfit us for the trip.

The fifth day of May we yoked our cattle, our cows and a pair or two of year-old steers; gathered up our scanty means; bought a few months' supplies; baby and I climbed into the wagon; the two gents mounted the seat in front; Mr. T. took the whip and we left the town of Zeandale with the determination of returning in the fall, or when we had made money enough to pay for the 160 acres of land and buy a little herd of cattle.

What I endured on the plains only those that crossed in '59 know. There was no station until we got to within 80 miles of D. [Denver] — no road a good part of the way. I was weak and feeble, having nearly shaken myself to death with fever and ague in Kansas. The Indians were all along the route, but friendly. But all Indians, like snakes, are the same to me. I lived in constant dread of them.

I had to cook for all our party and I did not find it a pleasure. Sometimes the wind would blow furiously and it is not very pleasant to cook over a camp fire in a wind storm when that fire is made of buffalo chips and every gust of wind would carry them over the barren prairie. By the time I would get them gathered together, another puff (and so on, lasting three or four days).

Every Sunday we rested, if rested it could be called. The men would go hunting, while I would cook, wash and iron, which kept me employed all day. My baby was teething and was sick all the way across, which, with my other work, made it hard for me.

We arrived in Denver somewhere between the 16th and 20th day of June, camped on the Platte River near where the West Side Bridge now stands. The cattle were footsore and we were obliged to stay until the 1st of July. Then we moved on up Clear Creek where the town of Golden now stands. Some one had come down from the Gregory Diggings from whom our men inquired the way to the Diggings.

Leaving me in the 7 x 9 tent to watch the cattle and keep them from straying, and with a baby to take care of, the three men took a supply of provisions upon their backs, a few blankets and telling me to be good to myself left on the Glorious Fourth. How sadly I felt, none but my God knew. Every morning and eve I had a round-up all to myself. There were no cowboys for me to shoot, cut and slash with then.

Three long, weary weeks I kept watch and ward. At the expiration of that time the men returned, and the 26th day of July we loaded up the wagon and started into the mountains. The road was a mere trail. At every few rods we were obliged to stop and widen the road so as to get the wagon through. Many hills we were obliged to take everything from the wagon and then help the oxen to get the wagon up, the men carrying the goods as best they could. In going down hill it was much easier, as it always is. We would often fasten a tree to the back of the wagon and drag it for a hold-back, or brake, down the hill. When night overtook us we were often in a place where we could not find a level place to spread our blankets. So we would drive stakes into the ground, roll a log against them, then lay with feet against the log and sleep, oh so sweetly, with Mother Earth for a bed and the blue sky for a roof.

We were nearly three weeks cutting our way down through Russell's Gulch, taking the first wagon through onto Pain's [sic] Bar, now known as Idaho [Idaho Springs]. We arrived there about the middle, or 20th of August. There was no woman there but many prospectors. The men cut trees or logs, laid them up four feet in height, mounted the tent on top for a roof, making me a comfortable 7 x 9 house.

Mr. T. went on to Spanish Bar and went prospecting. I opened an eating house; also made pies and bread to sell, and sold milk from the cows we had driven across the plains. I was very busy every moment from early morn until late at night, finding much more than busy hands could do.

With the 25th of September came the first snow, a few inches. An old Cal. miner came into camp and told Mr. T. that it would not do to keep a woman in the mountains in the winter. Said there would be fearful snow slides and we would be buried alive. Just think of it, you who have visited Idaho Springs. Snow slides from those foothills! Common sense ought to have told us better, but we had never seen a mountain, only as we passed through the Alleghanies en route West, and believing all an old miner would tell us, we pulled our tent and traveled toward Denver.

I had had what we called a profitable summer. I had made enough to pay for the farm and to keep us through the winter. Had found a trustworthy young man that would take the money and a dog that we had brought with us from home, one that I had raised back on the farm in Kansas. I did not feel able to feed the dog through the winter with the cheapest article of food that could be bought at 25 cents a pound and upward. So with many a sigh, I parted with my faithful "Petty."

Arriving at Denver, we took a room over Vasques' store. There was one window, a rough board floor, the roof reached to the floor — for which we paid $25 a month. The first house that I had been into for six months.

Mr. T. returned to his prospect hole and found it jumped. Might was right in those times. So he lost all his summer's time and had to sell the cow to raise money to get a new supply of groceries, as he wanted to go to a new camp that was much talked of.

The 14th day of February, 1860, we once more put our all into the wagon and I was lifted from a bed of sickness and laid upon the wagon and we left Denver, this time taking four men along. We drove out to a place about ten miles called Montana and camped. There were a few deserted huts, and we went into one for the night. No floor, no windows, nor door. I slept on the ground that night and awoke early, feeling better than when in Denver.

We were four days going down to where Manitou now stands. We camped near the Soda Springs and I mixed biscuits with some water. They were yellow and tasted so strongly of soda that we, with our outdoor appetites, did not relish them.

We lingered there one week, the men doing a little prospecting and some of them working upon the road up the Ute Pass. We started up into the mountains over the new road and for several days we made such slow progress that we could look back to the last night's camp smoke. The men worked hard to get the first wagon over the road. The weather was changeable, a few inches of snow falling nearly every night. I speak of this, for it made it wet and sloppy cooking over a camp fire, and my health was very poor that spring. We were two long, weary weeks getting up to the South Park. I shall never forget how beautiful the Park looked when I first beheld it. The sun was just setting, its beautiful rays reflected back, tinging the whole heavens with crimson and yellow clouds. It looked like a cultivated field with rivulets running through and herds of antelope; in the distance Weston Pass and I beheld and wondered and exclaimed, "Who made this, O God!"

Then we drove down and camped on the bank of a stream now called Jefferson Creek. The men went up the stream, and I went to washing soiled clothes in the clear, running creek. We wandered around in the Park several days, trying to find the tracks of a party of miners that had come in over Kenosha Hill. We knew them when they left Denver. They had a packed jack. We could find no trace of them.

About the fourth day in the Park, we came to Salt Creek late at night. We tried the water and found that we could not let the cattle drink from the stream. Neither could we use it ourselves. So another night we retired hungry and thirsty. The wind blew furiously, as it invariably does in the spring of the year over the Park. The night was cold, as usual in the Park. A jack came to our tent door and stood in the hot embers of the campfire until he singed his ankles and the odor that was wafted into our tent was anything but refreshing. The men drew their carbines and watched for guerillas, and many were the conjectures as to whom he belonged. He stayed with us to the end of our trip and hours he carried babe and myself on his back.

We moved on next day toward water and camped on Trout Creek. The men shouldered their muskets and went in search of our Denver friends, one man going each way. The one that found the party was to fire off his gun. All day long I listened for the report and when night came I felt desolate indeed, alone with a babe, without a dog. How bitterly I lamented having sent my "Petty" away. The jack came into the tent and laid down. I was even glad of his company. I laid my head down upon him and cried with loneliness. The men had gone farther than they thought before turning, and it was midnight before they found camp and would not have found it at all but for the fire I kept burning. They did not find the trail, so we concluded to follow the stream downward. . . . [Several pages of the account apparently are missing at this point.]

The river was rapid, with many large boulders, around which clung cakes of ice. We found what we thought was the best fording place and drove our oxen in. The water was icy cold. The cattle were thin, weak and tired and they halted in the middle of the river, and any amount of driving would not make them go. We "Whoa, Ha" and "Gee, Ha" but to no avail. The men plunged into that cold stream, which was waist deep, tied ropes to their horns, went onto the shore opposite and tried to drag them along. They were numb with cold and would not heed. The men were obliged to unload the wagon, putting the goods upon the ice, not knowing but it might move downward any moment; unyoke the cattle, drag the wagon over and the oxen, too, return and carry the goods. The faithful little jack carried baby and me, although he could only keep his nose above water.

We were six hours in crossing the Arkansas River. We started a camp fire and dried ourselves and nursed the cattle all night long. We felt that we must save them, for our supply of food was getting low and we should have to eat them before long. Stopping about this place a week or more, one man would fish, one hunt and the other would take a pan and shovel and wash out dirt, always finding a few specks of gold to a pan of dirt. Our evenings were passed in playing cards and relating home news.

Our next move was to follow up the river. After many hard days over steep, rocky hills, we camped where Cache Creek empties into the Arkansas. Here we pitched our tent and went to work in earnest. Mr. T. and Maxcy whip-sawed some [boards], made two sluice boxes, sawed riffles from a log, made a ditch from the creek and commenced to work the bank away. Cleaning the boxes up every night, we found plenty of fine gold but more black sand and being new at mining, knew no way to separate the gold from the sand only with the slow process of lifting the iron sand with a small magnet. Every day I would work hard trying to separate the metals and when night came I would weigh my day's worth and find that I had only a few pennyweights of gold. Four weeks we tarried and worked this way. Our provision was gone. We were depending upon the aim of our guns for food. Our bill of fare for breakfast was broiled venison, fried mountain sheep. Dinner: venison roast, boiled mountain mutton. Supper: Fried venison, baked sheep.

We were getting discouraged when one morning we saw a man coming toward camp, riding a jack, being attracted by our camp. Our prayer was that he could speak English. He arrived and seemed surprised to see a woman in camp. He told us to move on up 20 miles or more across the river and turn up a gulch after passing a huge bald mountain; that he was with a party that had found gold in paying quantities; that it was coarse and easily separated from the black sand. At first we were doubtful, but he showed about an ounce in small nuggets. Said that he was going for supplies.

The next morning we left the camp, loath to do so, for we well knew that if [we] were experienced miners we need look no further. We saw the bald mountain from the opposite side of the river, and plunged in. The river looked broad and shallow. When near the opposite bank, we came into a deep channel, our wagon bed raised above the wheels and floated down stream, myself and child in it. It was rapidly filling with water when the thought occurred to me to cling to the willows on the bank. I did so and held fast until the men who were coming on the shore rescued us. I knew nothing more until we were at the mouth of California Gulch.

We followed the stream up about six miles, passed the discoverers who were down on the stream at work while we were working our way through the thick timber.

This was the 8th day of May nearly three months since we left Denver. The first thing after we arrived was to kill the faithful old oxen that had brought us through and divide the beef with these miners that were there, they, too, being out of grub. Before night they had me a log cabin built. I think it was 12 x 18 feet — no door, nor window, no floor save the earth. I entered the place feeling queenly.

I at once commenced work, taking boarders, with nothing to eat but poor beef and dried apples. But this only lasted three days, for the man that had passed us en route for Denver met a pack train coming from New Mexico to Denver through the mountain pass. He persuaded them to go with him to the mountains with flour for which we paid $60 a sack, and it was one with sand.

We took our wagon bed to make some furniture, such as a table, sideboard, and the top to make three legged stools, to sit upon. But it mattered but little what we sat upon, for the only time that we sat down was when at our meals. There was work and good pay for it.

With the pack train that returned, word went that California Gulch had very rich diggings. Then came the rush of people. Before three months there were 10,000 people in the Gulch. A mail and express had been started — letters 75 cents each, express equally as high and they were kept at my cabin. Probably no other woman would be bothered with the crowd that it drew. I also had the only gold scales in the upper part of the Gulch, where we were centrally located, so I was called upon every evening to weigh gold dust for an hour or more.

When the men would clean up their sluice boxes for the day, they would go to town where Leadville now stands and gamble it all away, come home and try it again the next day. During the month from May to July, I weighed $80,000 worth of gold dust that was taken out of No. 20 above Discovery for Pat Wells and Jack Langon. Our claim was No. 21 above. I had the offer of No. 20, if I would board the owner for the summer when he was in the Gulch. He wanted to run an express from Denver.

When September came we had cleared $4000 from the diggings and my work. It seemed but little compared to what our neighbors had taken out. But it was so much more than we had ever had that we were satisfied.

Mr. Tabor gave me $1000 for my visiting expenses. I packed a carpet bag with my wardrobe, which had not been replenished since I left home. There had not been one dollar spent upon my wardrobe since I was married. Now three years and eight months, every dollar I had earned had gone to help make another.

I will state how the $1000 was used that was given me to go home with. As I went through Kansas, I purchased 160 acres of land adjoining that which we already owned, for which I paid $400. In the spring I bought a pair of horses and a wagon, which was $400 more. The other $200 paid my traveling expenses and my people dressed me up. Who can say that the money was squandered?

While we were in St. Joseph, Missouri buying the team and loading preparatory to another trip, the first gun was fired at Fort Sumter. Instead of turning back and volunteering we rushed on to get away from the war, which we knew had begun. (I thought of this last summer when General Logan reviewed his militia and Tabor was drawn around, dressed up in a brigadier's uniform and was driven in front of the procession.)

The spring was a cold one, and I had seven in family. At Fort Kearney we were quarantined for three days, while Uncle Sam took our teams and went 80 miles into the woods for wood for the soldiers.

The Indians were numerous and though assured that they were friendly, we were obliged to keep a watch out to keep them from driving off our stock. They would gather around our camp fire and whenever we were dining they would squat on the ground beside us, pick lice from their heads and from their children, crack them between their teeth and smile complacently at our disgust.

We were about the usual time, six weeks, crossing this time. The weather was very disagreeable. The women were cross, especially at meal time when they would have the flapjacks and bacon nearly ready and a strong wind would scatter them over the prairie. The men, of course, were always pleasant, and why should they not be on a trip like that, when their only ambition is to lay upon the grass and play cards while the women have the wood, a scarce article, to gather, the cooking and often the cattle to take care of? I do not wonder that men laugh and grow fat when they meditate how helpless women are cowed down by their iron will.

We undertook to pass the Western Range of mountains the first of April. The snow was four feet deep upon a level and packed very solid by the winds. For many days we shovelled and worked and at last got one empty team through. Then the miners turned out en masse and opened the road for us, hearing that there were four ladies with us. There was a grand banquet prepared for us on the even [sic] of our arrival. Hotel De Booth threw wide her doors to welcome us, having had no communication with the world outside for nearly six months, with dancing, banqueting, gambling and smoking all in the same room. The floor was puncheon, the music a fiddle, the lights tallow candles, a gambling table in each corner, where there was smoking. The wonderful supper! All it consisted of was beef, bread and dried apple sauce. There were warm hearts there and we were very happy to see the hospitality and kind feeling that was manifested toward us by the miners.

August the famous Philips Lode was discovered in Park County. There was a stampede from all parts of the country, and California Gulch being only 25 miles away, across Mosquito Range, many went there. So we, with the rest, packed up the remnants of our little store, put them into a wagon. I mounted a saddle mule, took the boy up behind and we started for the new Eldorado, bright with the hopes of doing better there.

When we were within a few miles of the top of the range, which lays between the waters of the Platte and those of the Arkansas, a fearful snow storm overtook us. We were not prepared to camp having intended to reach the top where a man kept a toll gate. We were obliged to stop just where we were, make our bed upon three feet of snow, cover a blanket over the top and retire. Strange to say, we slept soundly and only awoke whenever the covering of snow would press too heavily upon us. When morning dawned we found that the snow under us had settled and what we had rolled from our beds during the night had formed a bank three feet high, so our bed was comfortably warm; but we could not keep it, as the oxen had been tied to the wagon without any supper and we, too, were getting hungry.

(The manuscript ends here.)

Bibliography

Manuscript and Archival Material

Bancroft, Caroline, File. Denver: Western History Department, Denver Public Library.

Bartlett, A.T., Collection. St. Louis: St. Louis Historical Society.

Bradford, Robert, Letters. San Marino, CA: Huntington Library.

Bush, William, Papers. Denver: Western History Department, Denver Public Library.

Byers, Elizabeth, Papers. Denver: Western History Department, Denver Public Library.

Ellis Scrapbooks, I-IV. Denver: Western History Department, Denver Public Library.

Foote, Mary Hallock, Reminiscences. San Marino, CA: Huntington Library.

French, Adelaide, Collection. Denver: Western History Department, Denver Public Library.

Geiger, Marilyn L., "Zeandale Township, 1854-1896." Topeka, KS: Kansas State Historical Collection.

Kennedy, Marie C. "First 100 Years with the Denver Fire Department." Denver: Denver Fire Department Files.

Ladies' Aid Society, File. Denver: Unitarian Church.

Leadville City Guide. Denver: Writers' Program, 1940.

Machebeuf, Rev. Joseph, Papers. Denver: Catholic Archives, Archdiocese of Denver.

Mazzulla, Frances, Collection. Fort Worth, TX: Amon Carter Museum.

Mundkenk, Sarah, Collection. Denver: Western History Department, Denver Public Library.

Orahood, Harper, Papers. Boulder, CO: Western History Department, University of Colorado.

Perrigo, Lynn, "The Little Kingdom: A Record of Central City in the Early Days." Boulder, CO: Western History Department, University of Colorado.

Pillsbury, Josiah, Diary, 1850-1860. Manhattan, KS: Rare Books Room, Library of Kansas State University.

Riley County, Scrapbook. Manhattan, KS: Riley County Historical Museum.

Shakeshaft, Alston J., "The New England Legacy to Kansas." Topeka, KS: Ph.D. Thesis, Kansas State Historical Society.

Smith, Caroline Abbott, "A Sketch of the Early Days on Deep Creek." Manhattan, KS: Riley County Historical Museum.

Tabor, Augusta, Files. Denver: Western History Department, Denver Public Library.

Tabor, Elizabeth B., Files. Denver: Western History Department, Denver Public Library. Complete collection, Colorado Historical Society Library, Denver, CO.

Teller, Henry, Papers. Boulder, CO: Western History Department, University of Colorado.

Tritch, George, Papers. Denver: Western History Department, Denver Public Library.

Uzzell, Thomas, Collection. Denver: Western History Department, Denver Public Library.

Public Documents

Census Records
    State Census: Colorado, Kansas, Maine.
    Territorial Census: Colorado, Kansas.

Historical Plat Book of Riley County, Kansas, 1881.

Record Books, County Courthouses:
    Arapahoe County, Denver, Colorado.
    Kennebec County, Augusta, Maine.
    Lake County, Leadville, Colorado.
    La Plata County, Durango, Colorado.
    Park County, Fairplay, Colorado.
    Riley County, Manhattan, Kansas.

Books and Pamphlets

Bair, Everett, *This Will Be An Empire*. New York, NY: Pageant Press, 1959.

Bancroft, Hubert T., *Chronicles of the Builders*, Vol. 4. San Francisco: History Publishing Company, 1892.

Bean, Geraldine, *Charles Boettcher: A Study in Pioneer Western Enterprise*. Boulder, CO: Westview, 1976.

Beck, Joseph T., *Historical Notes on Augusta, Maine*. Farmington, MA: Knowlton & McLeary Co., 1962.

Blair, Edward, *Leadville: Colorado's Magic City*. Boulder, CO: Pruett Publishing Co., 1980.

Borden, W.W., *Leadville*. New Albany, IN: Cannon Publishing Co., 1879.

Brown, Dee, *The Gentle Tamers*. Lincoln, NE: University of Nebraska Press, 1958.

Coffin, Robert T., *Kennebec, Cradle of Americans*. New York: Farrar & Rinehart, 1937.

Davis, Clyde Brion, *The Arkansas*. New York: Farrar & Rinehart, 1940.

Dunning, Harold M., *Over Hill and Vale*, Vol. 2. Boulder, CO: Johnson Publishing Co., 1956-1962.

Farrow, Ella, *History of Holland*. Burlington, VT: Queen City Printers, 1979.

First One Hundred Years, A History of Manhattan, Kansas, 1855-1955. Manhattan, KS: Manhattan Centennial, Inc., 1955.

Fowler, William W., *Women on the American Frontier.* Hartford, CN: S.S. Scranton & Co., 1879.

Gandy, Lewis Case, *The Tabors: A Footnote of Western History.* New York: Press of the Pioneers, 1934.

Gillette, Ethel Morrow, *Idaho Springs: Saratoga of the West.* New York: Vantage Press, 1978.

Green, Charles R., *Early Days in Kansas.* Olathe, KS: C.R. Green, 1912-1914.

Griswold, Don and Jean, *Carbonate Camp Called Leadville.* Denver: University of Denver Press, 1951.

Hafen, Leroy, *Reports from Colorado, 1859-1865.* Glendale, CA: Arthur H. Clarke Co., 1961.

Hill, Alice Polk, *Tales of the Colorado Pioneers.* Glorietta, NM: Rio Grande Press, Inc., 1976.

Hollenbeck, Frank R., *Central City and Black Hawk, Then and Now.* Denver: Sage Press, 1961.

Howlett, Rev. W.J., *Life of the Rt. Rev. Joseph P. Machebeuf.* Pueblo, CO: 1908.

Huston, Fred, *Those S.O.B.'s at Tarryall.* Wichita Falls, TX: Nortex Press, 1974.

Jackson and Marshall, *Quest of the Snowy Cross.* Denver: University of Denver Press, 1952.

Johnson, Wallace S., *Autobiography.* Montana: Big Mountain Press, 1960.

Kennebec Journal, "Augusta's Centennial Souvenir, 1797-1897." Augusta, ME: 1897.

Kent, L.A., *Leadville*. Denver: Times Steam Printing House, 1880.

Kingsbury, Henry D., and Deyo, Simeon L., *Illustrated History of Kennebec County, Maine*. New York: H.W. Blake & Co., 1892.

Log Cabin Days. Manhattan, KS: Riley County Historical Society, 1929.

McConnell, Virginia, *Bayou Salado: The Story of South Park*. Denver: Sage Books, 1966.

Mumey, Nolie, *Amos Steck*. Denver: Sage Press, 1981.

Mumey, Nolie, *History and Proceedings of Buckskin Joe*. Boulder, CO: Johnson Press, 1961.

North, James W., *History of Augusta, Maine*. Somersworth, NH: New England History Press, 1981.

Richmond, Robert W., *Kansas: A Land of Contrasts*. St. Charles, MO: Forum Press, 1974.

Riley County Genealogical Society, *Pioneers of the Bluestream Prairie*. Manhattan KS: 1976.

Slagg, Winifred, *Riley County, Kansas*. Brooklyn, NY: Thomas Gauss Sons, 1968.

Smiley, Jerome. *History of Denver.* Denver: J. Williamson & Co., 1903.

Smith, Duane A., *Horace Tabor: His Life and the Legend*. Boulder, CO: Pruett Publishing Company, 1981.

Smith, Marion, *Westminster, Then and Now.* Westminster, CO: North Suburban Printing Co., 1976.

Spencer, Emma Dill Russell, *Gold Country, 1828-1858.* San Antonio, TX: Naylor Company, 1958.

Spencer, Emma Dill Russell, *Green Russell & Gold.* Austin, TX: University of Texas Press, 1966.

Stratton, Joanna L., *Pioneer Women.* New York: Touchstone Books, 1981.

Thomason, Matt, *Early History of Wabaunsee County, Kansas.* Alma, KS: 1901.

Time Life Series, *Pioneers* and *The Women.* New York: 1974-1978.

Vandenbusche, Duane, *Gunnison County.* Gunnison, CO: B & B Printers, 1980.

Voynick, Stephen M., *Leadville: A Miner's Epic.* Missoula, MT: Big Mountain Press, 1984.

Wiberg, Eloise Ruth, *Rediscovering Northwest Denver.* Boulder, CO: Pruett Publishing Co., 1976.

Williamson, Ruby G., *From Kansas to the Matchless.* Gunnison, CO: B & B Printers, 1975.

Willison, George, *Here They Dug the Gold.* London: Eyre & Spotteswoode, 1950.

Young, Bob and Jan, *Pike's Peak or Bust.* New York: Julius Messner, 1971.

Articles

Clarke, S.C., "Colorado and South Park." *Lippincott Magazine*, vol. 24, September 1873, pp. 332-338.

Flynn, Norma. "Early Mining Camps of South Park." *Colorado Magazine*, 1952.

Jackson, Helen Hunt, "To Leadville." *Atlantic Monthly*, vol. XLIII, May 1879, p. 575.

Sturm, Mayme G., "Mary York [Cozens], Pioneer Woman in Gregory Diggings." *Colorado Magazine*, vol. XXII, May 1945.

Wilson, John Taylor, "George Taylor: Augusta Tabor's Cousin." *Colorado Magazine*, vol. XXXIV, January 1957.

Newspapers and Periodicals

Central City Register Call
Colorado Magazine
Colorado Mining Gazette, Idaho Springs
Denver Post
Denver Republican
Denver Tribune
Durango Herald
Durango Record
Fairplay Flume
Golden Transcript
Gunnison Review Press
Hallowell (Maine) *Gazette*
Herald of Freedom
Idaho Springs News
Kanhistique (Ellsworth, Kansas)
Kansas Free State (Lawrence, Kansas)
Kansas Tribune (Topeka, Kansas)

Kennebec Journal
Lawrence (Kansas) *Journal-World*
Lawrence (Kansas) *Tribune*
Leadville Evening Chronicle
Leadville Herald-Democrat
Manhattan (Kansas) *Mercury-Chronicle*
Milwaukee Journal
Milwaukee Sentinel
Oshkosh Daily Journal
Pueblo Chieftain
Rocky Mountain Herald
Rocky Mountain News
St. Louis Republican
Squatter Sovereign (Atchison, Kansas)
Tarryall Miner
Trail Magazine
Wichita Eagle

Pierce Genealogy

William Babcock Pierce	Lucy Eaton (Pierce)
Born: October 20, 1804	*Born:* June 10, 1805
Died: March 27, 1873	*Died:* May 22, 1875

Married: November 13, 1828

Rebecca Foster
Born: August 27, 1829   *Died:* January 9,1899
Married: P.J. Folsom, February 22, 1852

Melvina Lucy
Born: April 28, 1831   *Died:* August 2, 1896
Married: Arthur C. Clark, March 30, 1861

Augusta Louise
Born: March 29, 1833   *Died:* January 30, 1895
H.A.W. Tabor, January 31, 1857

Vesta
Born: January 13, 1835   *Died:* May 30, 1855

Ruthe Elizabeth
Born: September 29, 1836   *Died:* September 1, 1907
Married: F.D. Peterson, November 6, 1865

Edwin (William H.)
Born: September 26, 1838   *Died:* December 25, 1894
Married: Frances Saben, May 28, 1859

Nahum Franklin
Born: July 2, 1840   Died: March 17, 1909
Married: Flora Moody, January 19, 1871

Mary Frances
Born: April 15, 1842   *Died:* June 10, 1899
Married: C.H. Marston, June 28, 1862

Lilly T.
Born: April 22, 1844   *Died:* May 16, 1925
Married: C.F. Taylor, February 13, 1867

Fred Marshall
Born: June 23, 1846   *Died:* September 10, 1894
Married: Mary Yeaton, January 4, 1873

Index

COLORADO PROFILES:
Men and Women Who Shaped the Centennial State
John H. Monnett and Michael McCarthy
   340 pp., photos, (6 x 9), ISBN: 0-917895-19-3, softcover, $14.95

GUIDE TO HISTORIC DURANGO & SILVERTON
Duane A. Smith
   48 pp., photos, maps, (7½ x 9), ISBN: 0-917895-16-6,
   softcover, $4.95

GUIDE TO HISTORIC CENTRAL CITY & BLACK HAWK
Sarah J. Pearce and Christine Pfaff
   48 pp., photos, maps, (7½ x 9), ISBN: 0-917895-15-0,
   softcover, $4.95

GUIDE TO THE GEORGETOWN-SILVER PLUME
HISTORIC DISTRICT
   48 pp., photos, maps, (7½ x 9), ISBN: 0-917895-08-8,
   softcover, $4.95

ROOF OF THE ROCKIES: A History of Colorado Mountaineering
William M. Bueler
   264 pp., photos, maps, (5½ x 8½), ISBN: 0-917895-06-1,
   softcover, $12.95

SKI TRACKS IN THE ROCKIES: A Century of Colorado Skiing
Abbott Fay
   100 pp., photos, (8½ x 10½), ISBN: 0-917895-02-9,
   softcover, $10.95